# Redesigning Supervision

# Redesigning Supervision

## ALTERNATIVE MODELS FOR STUDENT TEACHING AND FIELD EXPERIENCES

*Adrian Rodgers and Deborah Bainer Jenkins*

*with Robert V. Bullough, Jr., C. J. Daane, M. Winston Egan, Cheryl Fortman, Virginia L. Keil, Jeffrey D. Nokes, and Elizabeth K. Wilson*

FOREWORD BY KENNETH R. HOWEY

TEACHERS COLLEGE PRESS

Teachers College, Columbia University
New York and London

Published by Teachers College Press, 1234 Amsterdam Avenue, New York, NY 10027

*Library of Congress Cataloging-in-Publication Data*

Rodgers, Adrian.
   Redesigning supervision : alternative models for student teaching and field experiences / Adrian Rodgers and Deborah Bainer Jenkins ; with Robert V. Bullough . . . [et al.] ; foreword by Kenneth R. Howey.
      p.   cm.
   Includes bibliographical references and index.
   ISBN 978-0-8077-5060-5 (pbk : alk. paper)
   1. Student teaching—United States—Planning.   2. Student teachers—Supervision of—United States.   I. Jenkins, Deborah Bainer.   II. Title.

   LB2157.U5R64 2010
   370.71'1—dc22

                                                                        2009047693

ISBN 978-0-8077-5060-5 (paper)

Printed on acid-free paper
Manufactured in the United States of America

17   16   15   14   13   12   11   10       8   7   6   5   4   3   2   1

We dedicate this book to students of teaching, both yours and ours, who challenge our assumptions about teaching, who inspire lifelong learning, and with whom we love to work.

# Contents

**PART III**
**The Implications of Using Alternative Models**

# Foreword

I have studied a variety of approaches to teacher preparation for over four decades now. Despite a growing corpus of knowledge to support what is enabling to prospective teachers, debate remains about how widely such practices exist across the broad array of programs preparing teachers. What is not debatable, however, is the widespread, woeful state of clinical and student teaching support provided prospective teachers. Far too often, preparation programs have difficulty recruiting outstanding veteran teachers to supervise their prospective teachers. This should be little wonder given that these programs typically provide few incentives in the way of monetary support, title and privileges, release time, or leadership and professional development designed to enhance and enrich their supervisory abilities. Further, many teachers in their high-stakes environment harbor major reservations about taking on another responsibility or having "new recruits" teach in their classrooms.

On the other side of the ledger, far too many college professors and instructors similarly shun supervisory duties. They cite a heavy teaching load or nominal consideration of supervision in tenure and promotion decisions as reasons for avoiding such responsibilities. Often, neither party has any deep understanding of effective supervisory practice. For example, I have a colleague who advocates an excellent clinical model that begins with exposition in a college classroom. That classroom instruction is complemented by individual demonstration teaching in a PreK-12 classroom utilizing the same practices promoted in the lecture hall. The process then extends to providing scaffolding to and structuring guided practice for the novice teacher. The clinical model ultimately culminates in a rigorous examination of how the prospective teacher's instruction impacted her or his students, employing a variety of student work examples. I could easily endorse such a model, but I have yet to witness it in practice.

I have no doubt that the linchpin to needed reforms in the preparation of teachers will be the close, collaborative efforts of boundary-spanning individuals, such as the contributors to this book, who are truly vested in and knowledgeable about the clinical preparation of prospective teachers.

Rodgers, Bainer Jenkins, and their colleagues have stepped squarely into the breach and have provided us with an extremely helpful book. They not only point us in new directions, they provide specifics for how to get there.

Upon reflection, I find this book is grounded in four informative domains. First, given the authors' rich experiences, they provide insight into how to redress the host of *practical* problems that beset both student teaching and its supervision. The confluence of three distinctive cultures alone guarantees a long list of answers to "What do I do now?"

Second, the book provides three detailed cases, which chronicle alternatives to the pervasive university supervisor/school cooperating teaching format. The strength of these cases is their realism—and the authors' candid portrayal of the problems, as well as the successes, encountered over time. We hear why some elements of these alternative approaches didn't work and what can be done to address these problems.

Third, the book extends the provocative theoretical and empirical frameworks for planned change developed by Michael Fullan to guide a cross-case analysis (see Chapter 6). Along one dimension, structural and programmatic aspects are examined, and along a second, cultural and reculturing challenges are examined. The former addresses such core problems as finding time to meet together. The latter explores, for example, how to develop better understanding and respect for individuals working in quite different professional cultures and with many aspects of their complex work not all that transparent.

Fourth, the authors draw from diverse literature over time, as well as their considerable experience, to address specific understandings, abilities, and dispositions needed to provide high quality supervision for beginning teachers. This is particularly helpful since the core activities of supervision are far too often addressed at a level of generality that is less than useful.

In closing, I wish to express my appreciation for being asked to write a brief foreword. It is an honor. I learned a good deal in reading, and rereading, this book—and had it proven to me that these authors can "teach an old dog new tricks."

—Kenneth R. Howey

# Acknowledgments

This book shares the work of faculty, teachers, and student teachers collected over a decade. All the authors are deeply grateful for the support of children, school staffs, schools, and districts for being willing to host faculty and their students and for making us feel at home in their schools.

We appreciate the support of our colleagues and colleges of education who have been supportive personally and professionally by being intrigued by and supportive of our innovative designs. Adrian is also appreciative of a grant provided by The Ohio State University at Newark for the completion of this book.

The idea for this book came about when Adrian was finishing his work with the Urban Network to Improve Teacher Education (UNITE) and starting a faculty position at The University of Toledo in the mid-1990s. At UNITE Adrian had the privilege of working closely with Ken Howey and meeting Michael Fullan, who have both had a profound impact on innovative design and the challenges it poses. At The University of Toledo Adrian was lucky enough to have the support of Ginny Keil, who was excited to try alternative approaches to school partnership.

This book would not have been possible without the support of five sets of individuals or teams. Debbie Bowman helped all of the contributing authors with the mechanics of preparing the manuscript. The families of the authors were also great sources of inspiration, support, and patience. Thank you, Emily, for all your help. Adrian is most grateful for the kind support of his co-author Deb Bainer Jenkins, who first introduced him to the field of teacher education in 1994, and who continued to shape the thinking behind this book in the prospectus, outlining, and writing. There are few people whom you can talk to all day long for three days in a row as ideas are hatched, so there is little wonder that Deb's sound reasoning and supportive voice is woven throughout this book. We are also most grateful for the work of The University of Alabama and the Brigham Young University research teams, who were gracious in sharing their work. Our deepest gratitude goes to readers like you, who we hope will find this book a useful guide in attempting your own redesign initiatives. We look forward to reading and hearing about your efforts.

# CHAPTER 1

# Overview: Making a Case for Alternative Models

*Adrian Rodgers*

S TUDENTS AND UNIVERSITY faculty generally agree that field experiences are an essential part of teacher preparation (Calderhead & Shorrock, 1997; Grossman, 1990; Howey & Zimpher, 1989; Poser, 1996), but the way these experiences are supervised has remained essentially unchanged for over 50 years (Anderson, 1992; Hayes et al., 1996). This lack of change is surprising, given the increased calls for accountability in education (National Commission on Teaching for America's Future, 1996), renewed interest in educational reforms (Holmes Group, 1995), and the innovation of Professional Development Schools, which one might think would lead to reforms (Fullan, Galluzzo, Morris, & Watson, 1998; Holmes Group, 1990). Although the seascape of teacher education and initial teacher preparation is changing (Beck & Kosnik, 2006; Zeichner, Melnick, & Gomez, 1996), the traditional model for teacher supervision remains largely unchanged.

Historically, alternatives to the traditional supervision model have existed (Anderson, 1992; Partington, 1982), but the traditional triad based on the work of Cogan, Goldhammer, and Anderson remains by far the most common approach (as cited in Costa & Garmston, 1994). Although the traditional supervision model remains untouched, a number of issues are at work in the currents of change that compose the seascape of teacher education. These issues necessitate the reconsideration of how supervision is structured. Although there are many issues informing teacher education, there are four in particular that inform thinking regarding teacher preparation generally and preservice teacher supervision specifically:

1. Preservice teachers bring a range of backgrounds to learning to teach (Dill, 1996), which might not be fully accommodated in a traditional model in which one size fits all.

2. Cooperating teachers are asked to take on an increasing number
   of roles in initial and ongoing teacher preparation including supervising (Kent, 2001; Veal & Rickard, 1998), mentoring (Achinstein &
   Athanases, 2006; Correia & McHenry, 2002; Fairbanks, Freedman, &
   Kahn, 2000; Hunter & Kiernan, 2005; Portner, 2005), collaborating
   (Carroll, 2002), and establishing communities of reflective practice
   (McEntee et al., 2003); but they are asked to complete the same procedures for field placements.
3. University supervisors occupy different statuses, including those
   of negotiator (Slick, 1998b), disenfranchised outsider (Slick, 1998a),
   and hard-pressed faculty member (Beck & Kosnik, 2002), but they
   must complete the same paperwork and procedures for everyone
   they supervise, regardless of the preservice teacher's skill level or
   background.
4. Schools provide multiple contexts, including those of caring communities (Yusko, 2004), instructional practice communities (Supovitz, 2002), and professional communities (Lord, 1994; Street,
   2004); but they must accommodate the same triad in the same time
   period with the same documentation requirements for everyone
   they supervise, regardless of the preservice teacher's skill level or
   background.

Clearly, the changing nature of the individuals and settings engaged in
supervision receives little consideration within the traditional supervision
structure.

Kuhn (1970) suggested that when an individual works within existing
systems, that individual is "a solver of puzzles, not a tester of paradigms."
This is because the individual in a system may "try out a number of alternative approaches," but because of systemic limitations "he is not testing the
paradigm when he does so" (p. 109). What is needed is a redesign effort by
teacher educators willing to stretch existing paradigms or even work outside them—not because supervision is broken, but because the context for
supervision is changing and because teacher educators can now capitalize
on decades of research. Wilson and Daviss (1994) suggest that

> an effective redesign infrastructure in education would develop, test, refine,
> and integrate reforms. It would contract with a school or district . . . [and]
> would itself be constantly engaged in redesign to make its own programs
> better, more useful, and more cost-efficient. (p. 47)

Such redesign efforts could be measured by their ability to capitalize on
success, improve quality, expand usefulness, and keep costs low (p. 30).

Not all the alternatives that we report in this book have been tested so fully, and even the alternatives that have been extensively tested have been tested in only one area of the country. Therefore, the contributors to this book do not claim that the traditional supervision structures should be abandoned in favor of these alternative models. If the traditional supervision model might be considered Supervision 1.0, the work shared here represents not Supervision 2.0 or 3.0, but Supervision 1.3.

Although the contributors have had some success, readers of this book should not think redesign is easy or quick. Scholars who write about redesign teach us that redesign efforts are often messy (Fullan, 2007), are likely to have failures (Sarason, 1990), and of necessity should take a "ready-fire-aim" approach (Fullan, 1993, p. 31). Rather than being derisive of redesign efforts, Fullan means by "ready-fire-aim" that stakeholders need to prepare themselves for reform, need to actually initiate the reform, and then need to hone and refine the initial efforts. Thus, the alternatives proposed in this book might be considered as a part of the *fire* phase of redesign—initial attempts reported to a readership interested in building on, honing, and taking to scale the change they might find useful.

Useful designs need to be brought to scale and employed alongside traditional models so teacher educators can choose from a range of options to meet the needs of different constituents. To begin this redesign effort, we offer here three fundamentally different ways to organize field experiences. We consider what might be gained from this reorganization and discuss the issues related to such changes. It is the hope of all the contributors that readers consider the usefulness of the alternatives suggested and then deliberate about whether the alternatives or variations could be piloted locally. Readers should view these test pilots as only one way of addressing the changing and wide-ranging needs of those invested in preparing high-quality teachers. In this way, the scholarship and redesign of supervision might move from *fire* to *aim* and be better targeted at supporting a customized relationship between stakeholders in initial teacher preparation.

## SOME ESSENTIAL QUESTIONS ABOUT FIELD EXPERIENCES

Teacher educators are very interested in change and reform. For example, a series offered by the publisher of this book, Teachers College Press, is titled Series on School Reform. One of the problems inherent in this focus is that new ideas are easily adopted without careful consideration. These ideas often fail, perhaps because careful consideration of their design was not undertaken from the outset, and teacher educators are left to brainstorm new ideas again (Sarason, 1990). If teacher educators are to embark

on redesign, it is essential that questions about how field experience works
and how it might be changed be posed:

- Who are the people involved in supervision and what do they do?
- How are preservice teachers traditionally supported?
- Who are the members of the traditional support structure and how
  does that complicate quality supervision?
- What is the plan for this book to examine alternatives?

The following sections discuss these questions as part of redesigning field
experiences.

## Who Are the People Involved in Supervision and What Do They Do?

When we attend academic conferences or read scholarly papers on supervision, we usually can understand what the authors mean when they use
particular terms. There are occasions, however, when we need to ask a
quick question to clarify the terms an author has used. Since our readership might range beyond the typical audience of teacher educators at a
conference, we offer definitions of key terms. These definitions are not
standardized, and we have learned that for some, usage can differ across
locations, especially across different countries. The following definitions
reflect the language we will use to describe the three sets of key stakeholders we describe. In addition to these definitions, further stakeholders
and some key recurring terms have been identified, and these are defined
and discussed in a glossary at the end of the book.

*Preservice Teachers.* Preservice teachers are enrolled in course work
at a college or university that is part of a teacher preparation program. These
individuals could be at any point in their preparation program and may
be enrolled as undergraduates in the 1st, 2nd, 3rd, or 4th year or as graduate students, or as students with a degree who are taking additional course
work. Preservice teachers do not yet have a teaching credential but are
earning one and are sometimes also called *candidates* or *teacher candidates*
to reflect their uncredentialed status. We decided not to use the term
*teacher candidates*, preferred by the National Council for Accreditation of
Teacher Education (NCATE) (see www.ncate.org), partly because not
every teacher preparation institution in the United States is affiliated with
NCATE and partly because this is a term less used outside the United
States. The preservice teachers' principal task is to learn about teaching
through course work and field experiences. There are also outlier groups

of preservice teachers, including those who are enrolled in alternative teacher preparation programs, such as individuals enrolled in initial teacher preparation courses who are already employed as teachers in high-need areas.

*Cooperating Teachers.* These are individual teachers working in schools who have volunteered to host one or more preservice teachers in their classrooms. In public schools, cooperating teachers would often have a teaching credential; in private schools, teacher educators often seek cooperating teachers who have a teaching credential. Teacher preparation institutions may set a minimum standard, such as a couple of years of teaching experience, for cooperating teachers. The cooperating teacher—called the CT, or "coop"—is expected to provide opportunities for the preservice teacher to lead the class, especially in the middle and later field experiences; to assist the preservice teacher in planning lessons; to authorize the teaching of those lessons; and to provide formative and summative feedback. Formative feedback are notes and commentary intended to change a preservice teacher's teaching; summative feedback is a description of the achievements of preservice teachers, often for the purpose of making a decision on whether they can proceed, whether they successfully fulfilled the field experience, or whether they can be recommended for a teaching credential. Cooperating teachers often receive very little in return. Sometimes cooperating teachers have a positive experience in working with preservice teachers, which supports growth and depth in the field experience. At other times, preservice teachers require considerable supervision, and preservice teachers who have difficulty in their first attempts at teaching can take up large amounts of the cooperating teacher's time. Cooperating teachers may receive a very small stipend—in the 100s of dollars—or they or their school may receive a fee waiver or tuition reduction so that a cooperating teacher or another teacher can enroll in university course work at reduced or no cost. Often cooperating teachers volunteer their services as a duty to the profession or to work with a different group of educators. (For different case studies, see Doepker, 2007.)

*University Supervisors.* University supervisors are individuals employed by the university to oversee a group of preservice teachers. They typically visit the preservice teacher at the school, observe the preservice teacher teach a class, confer with both the preservice teacher and cooperating teacher individually and together, and provide formative and summative feedback to the preservice teacher with a copy for the cooperating teacher. Since the university supervisor sees multiple individuals in multiple settings, his or her key tasks are to take a developmental perspective in supporting the preservice teacher, to inform the cooperating teacher of institutional expectations, and to protect the integrity of the program by ensuring that standards are met. A university supervisor might make only a couple of visits to the field for a preservice teacher in an early field experience and 5–10 visits to a preservice teacher in later field experiences. The university supervisor acts as a liaison between all other parties and addresses problems. Typically the university supervisor either assigns a letter grade or pass/fail grade to the preservice teacher or determines a grade in consultation with the cooperating teacher.

*Other Stakeholders.* In addition to the above groups of stakeholders, there are other individuals described in this book, and there are more nuanced terms used to describe the individuals above. These terms are defined in the Glossary.

In the section above we focused on helping readers understand the role and importance of key stakeholders. In the next chapter we will consider what research has found regarding these same roles. Now, let's consider how preservice teachers are supported.

### How Are Preservice Teachers Traditionally Supported?

Field experience is seen by all teacher educators as an essential part of teacher preparation (McIntyre, Byrd, & Fox, 1996) because it provides novice teachers with opportunities for professional growth (for cases, see Calderhead & Shorrock, 1997 or Grossman, 1990) and provides opportunities for knowledgeable others such as cooperating teachers and university supervisors to influence and shape beginners (for strategies, see Sullivan & Glanz, 2000). Even educational critics who have been openly vocal of college teacher-preparation programs advocate the usefulness of supervised field experience (Conant, 1963; Reiman & Thies-Sprinthall, 1998). Traditionally, supervised field experiences provide preservice teachers with an opportunity to practice teaching under supervision in the safety of a supportive environment. The nature of these experiences differ depending on the teacher preparation program but can include early, middle, and later experiences (Anderson & Radencich, 2001). The middle-level experiences may be partnered with campus courses that examine different teaching methods. These methods courses and middle-level field experiences might be scheduled a year to a semester prior to the end of the teacher preparation program. Typically the later field experience, often placed in the last term of teacher preparation, is student teaching. Frequently this experience has limited campus course work, freeing the student teacher to work in schools and concentrate on teaching.

Both the middle and later field experiences almost always have significant supervision components built into them, and the three individuals who undertake this work—the preservice teacher, the cooperating teacher, and the university supervisor—are known collectively as the *supervision triad*. The preservice teacher is supported by at least one cooperating teacher who hosts the preservice teacher in his or her class. The cooperating teacher can fill many roles, but borrowing from Wang and Odell's (2002) review of the literature on mentoring, cooperating teachers often may see themselves as local guides who help a preservice teacher through the apprenticeship into teaching. In other words, the cooperating teacher serves as a support for preservice teachers as they become part of a professional community (Street, 2004; Yusko, 2004). Examples of this support include assistance in lesson planning as well as a deep, highly local understanding of the ins and outs of how those lessons will work with a particular group of students at a particular time of day.

An additional support for the student teacher is the university supervisor. The university supervisor visits the preservice teacher periodically and during these visits performs a number of tasks (Slick, 1998a, 1998b). A primary task is observing the preservice teacher and documenting those observations. Observations can be shared with the preservice teacher both for the purpose of improving and obtaining insight into instruction and for the purpose of making decisions on whether the preservice teacher can continue in the program. During these visits the university supervisor also supports the development of a quality relationship between the cooperating teacher and the preservice teacher. The university supervisor often debriefs experiences both individually with the preservice teacher and the cooperating teacher and with them together as members of the triad. Finally, the university supervisor acts as a liaison between the university and the triad members both to ensure that university requirements are met and to resolve issues. Because the triad ensures that the interests of all stakeholders are represented, it is not surprising that the supervision triad has been around for more than 50 years as a part of teacher induction in American education.

### Who Are the Members of the Traditional Support Structure, and How Does That Complicate Quality Supervision?

The supervision triad is both common and time tested, so much so that teacher educators tend to see it as de facto for preparing preservice teachers for the profession. Although the triad is commonplace, each member brings different knowledge, skills, and dispositions to supervision, and they must negotiate these within their professional roles and the limitations posed by their professional setting and culture. In this section we discuss these challenges.

Despite the changing face of teacher preparation, the supervision triad has remained largely unaltered. In an age of increasing educational accountability, it is immunized from reform efforts. While its popularity clearly indicates that it is useful and that it works, let's consider in more detail the work of triad members and how this complicates supervision. For the purpose of illustration and discussion, we adopt the rhetorical strategy of creating fictional characters who are composites based on educators with whom we've worked or whose work has been related to us by others. It is our hope that in these composite characters, readers will recognize themselves and their peers and will sympathize with the real problems and constraints faced by teacher educators in the preparation of teachers.

***Different Individuals Working Within a Single Model.*** Western Pacific University (WPU) is a comprehensive institution located at the hub of the twin cities of Western Way and Pacific Outlook, somewhere in the Pacific Northwest. The twin cities, which most residents abbreviate as WestPac, constitute a medium-sized metropolis dominated by its university. Over 25,000 students attend WPU, and its College of Education has a large number of undergraduate students seeking their initial teaching credential and a large number of master's students who are already credentialed teachers. The college also features a couple of small doctoral programs in instructional leadership and school counseling.

Demetria is the head of the Student Teaching Office. She retired after 30 years of teaching and serving as a principal at a nearby school. Interested in keeping active in education, she saw this new job as a way of supporting her profession and keeping in contact with her many colleagues in the area. As a lifelong learner, Demetria enrolled part time in the college's doctoral leadership program and is now halfway through her course work.

When Demetria began teaching more than 3 decades ago, her own teacher preparation program was dominated by a group that she learned was the traditional face of beginning teachers: White, 20-something women who were raised in suburban blue-collar homes and who wanted to teach in the same schools they had attended as children. Nowadays, especially because of the expansion of satellite campuses that WPU had established in strip malls across the tricounty region, Demetria finds that students seeking admission to the teacher credential program are much more diverse. Students are likely to be older—women who have raised their children and want to enter the workforce, single moms seeking a career, and unemployed single dads who have lost jobs in the economic downturn. Since some students have completed or partially completed undergraduate degrees years ago, the review of applicants is now more complex. Demetria has even reviewed applications from one or two attorneys and from English PhDs who wanted to work with children.

Demetria has not considered any range of supervision options, so WPU uses the same supervision triad model exclusively in early and middle field experiences and in student teaching as it did 30 years ago. The name "Student Teaching Office" is inaccurate, since Demetria and her staff place students in both field experiences connected to methods courses and in student teaching. Demetria likes that she has some freedom to assign field placements for students. Faculty occasionally add notes to student teaching applicants' files such as "This student would do well in a lower grades placement" or "This student would do well with a highly structured cooperating teacher"—a code that Demetria knows means a cooperating teacher with a no-nonsense approach. Although Demetria gives careful consideration to faculty notes, she often considers but dismisses student notes. Students often implore her for placements in schools they had attended as children or for placements in the wealthy suburb of Mountainview. Demetria noticed that only three students had ever asked to be placed at City Center School, in the downtown core, and she has learned from some colleagues that City Center has so many "issues" it simply does not make for a good placement. Demetria tries to support city schools by placing the students who wanted to student teach downtown at the nearby City Ridge school. Although Demetria has some control over grade and building placement, she exercises little control over anything else. In fact, a couple of school districts have contractual requirements that specify that student teachers be placed with cooperating teachers who have the most seniority, not always an optimal match.

Although Demetria does not always have as much control over placement as she would like, she does have a little more choice regarding the supervisors she assigns to a particular student and placement. Al, Babette, Casey, and Doug are four of the many supervisors she works with. Al (or "Old Al," as everyone calls him) is an adjunct instructor at WPU and had actually been Demetria's cooperating teacher when she was student teaching. Everyone calls him Old Al because he has a son, Young Al, who had taught at the same school as Old Al until Old Al's retirement from teaching 3 years ago. Because Al had taught for 40 years, he receives an indexed pension equivalent to 100% of his teaching salary, which Demetria knows must be over $80,000. She was surprised a couple of years ago when she was desperate for an additional supervisor and he agreed to accept $400 per student to supervise eight students (see sample compensation rates in

Doepker, 2007). Demetria was initially worried that because of this low pay, Al might do the least supervision work possible, but she found that he enjoyed being in schools and seeing old friends, and he undertook his new job with relish. On the other hand, Al is sometimes confused about the assignments the methods instructors on campus create for the field experience students he supervises, and he is never quite sure how to respond to students who seem to use excessive small-group work when whole-class direct instruction would seem to be more efficient.

Babette is one of the few full-time doctoral students at WPU and works as a graduate assistant, primarily supervising field experience and student teachers. Babette had taught English in her home province of Quebec and then moved to downtown Vancouver, British Columbia, where she taught French immersion. Not only fluent in English and French, Babette had also learned some Mandarin from her students when she was teaching in Vancouver's Chinatown. Interested in the role teachers could play in leadership, she applied to a number of doctoral programs, but she opted for WPU, since her assistantship covered the full cost of tuition and included a stipend for living expenses.

Although Babette was well versed in issues of cultural and linguistic diversity and had moved only a few hundred miles to attend graduate school, her move to the United States produced culture shock. Because of her inability to speak Spanish, she never felt she fully connected with some of the linguistic issues in the rural schools where her students were placed; these schools had an influx of children of Hispanic migrant laborers. She was also surprised that district residents did not support that children learn Spanish and English, preferring that children master their second language, English, first.

Babette was committed to her work and had taken doctoral course work in supervision, but she was still annoyed at some of the practices she saw at WPU. She felt that some university faculty seemed obsessed by their exclusive focus on state standards. In fact, she recently asked her students to write their own lesson plan objectives, and the best they could do was copy a state standard from the state department of education's Web site. Although Babette was licensed to teach K–12 French and K–8 English in two Canadian provinces, she did not have an American teaching credential, a fact that she carefully hid from her students and from cooperating teachers. Although she could provide excellent feedback to middle-grade English and French teachers, she also frequently found herself observing a middle-grade science lesson or a first-grade reading lesson, and these were observations that she felt really tested her ability to provide any useful feedback. Babette was also annoyed that WPU let her office mate, Babs, do the same work that she did. Babs had earned a bachelor's and master's degree in Renaissance literature from WPU and had taught successfully at the exclusive, private Ocean Country Day School for a number of years. Although Babs had never taken an education course, let alone completed a teaching credential, she enrolled in the doctoral program in education, and because the program was short on supervisors with teaching experience, she also supervised students. Although Babette knew that Babs was bright and had some teaching skills, Babette felt that Babs never really understood how to put knowledge into action, the concept of pedagogical reasoning that she had recently read about in the classic article by Shulman (1987).

Casey had been a full-time school teacher and part-time doctoral student at WPU 20 years ago. She kept switching back and forth between the counseling and the leadership programs, but she lost interest in finishing the degree after her advisor retired. Ten years ago, partly in response to NCATE mandates for closer collaboration with schools, WPU arranged an exchange-of-services agreement with a local school district whereby they would pay for an entry-year teacher to replace Casey, and Casey would earn her full teaching salary but teach at the university. Everyone liked the arrangement and although Casey is still on leave from her school, she has taught as a full-time lecturer at WPU for over a decade. Casey is well liked by students and seems to have the ability to teach anything, so she is often the go-to person when an extra section of a course is created at the last minute. The remainder of her load is filled with supervision duties.

Doug is an assistant professor who was hired 5 years earlier and is going up for tenure next year. After a short but highly successful teaching career highlighted by a state teaching award, Doug opted to pursue doctoral studies so he could learn more about teaching. When he joined the faculty at WPU, he took the time to get to know his colleagues and was surprised to learn that half of his peers, especially those in educational foundations, did not hold a teaching credential. Since his colleagues in educational history, philosophy, and psychology did not seem to have taught in schools, he also learned that it was up to him and a few colleagues who taught methods courses to round out the pool of supervisors. Doug was challenged by his recent role as a faculty member. He learned that some of his senior colleagues had little respect for supervision, which was a double-edged sword: As a newer colleague, senior faculty expected Doug to supervise, but they also expected prolific scholarship and Doug's scholarly interests were not connected to the field. Even after just 5 years Doug finds that he is loosing his connection to schools, and he wonders how senior faculty can supervise students with any real credibility, since they do so very rarely. Doug also notices that when he speaks to students he sometimes talks over their heads. He has to keep reminding himself that they are beginners and that they do not have the experience and depth of knowledge that he has. Most annoying to Doug is that Demetria has assigned him to supervise one student teacher on the east side of WestPac and another on the west side. He was, Demetria had told him, the only person with expertise in middle-childhood science and while that was true, he knew nothing about mathematics, which was a second concentration of both students. Considering he was being reimbursed 50 cents a mile, he was wracking up great mileage, but he found he was spending 2 hours on the road for every trip to both schools, and this was taking a toll on his scholarly productivity. The dean of education at WPU had assured him that only publication in blind, peer-reviewed journals should count as scholarship for tenure, and Doug found himself beginning to resent each trip to the schools, an experience he had previously loved. Although he was by nature cheerful and well meaning, he wondered more and more, "Am I just another Casey who earns half the money and has twice the number of college degrees and student debt?"

*Complications of Individuals with Different Backgrounds Working Within a Single Model.* While Demetria enjoys the strength of a pool of supervisors with vastly different experiences, these differences raise a number of issues when individuals must work within a single model. Clearly, the considerable degrees of local knowledge and experience that adjunct faculty, especially those who are retired teachers, bring to supervision is highly valued, but it also raises some issues. One challenge is that adjunct faculty may be so rooted in the field that they are out of touch with what occurs on campus. This disconnect may then manifest itself in the kinds of feedback an adjunct faculty member provides to a preservice teacher. In an era that emphasizes partnerships between schools and universities, a second challenge is the issue of having adjunct faculty as the principal face of the university in schools.

The use of graduate students as supervisors also raises some interesting challenges. Clearly the teaching experiences and depth of content knowledge that both Babette and Babs bring to supervision are valuable assets, as is their recent teaching in public and private schools. Despite these assets, Babette recognizes some of the challenges. In a profession where educators rely on highly localized forms of knowledge, both Babs and Babette certainly will take some time to adjust to their new setting as they become accustomed to the philosophy and expectations of a different setting. A second challenge for graduate students is that while they may have recent and relevant teaching experience, this does not necessarily mean they are good supervisors. As readers shall see, quality supervision calls on a different skill set from that of teaching, and the two do not necessarily go hand in hand. Providing developmentally appropriate feedback to a preservice teacher is different from teaching children, and exercising care to make suggestions that are on the edge of a preservice teacher's understanding so that the suggestions are neither too easy nor too hard to accomplish is a skill that takes time to develop. Many graduate assistants take 3 or 4 years to develop these skills but then leave the university on the completion of their degree.

The benefits of Casey's employment arrangement are considerable for the university: It gets a teacher whose salary it could probably not afford, but only incurs the cost of a junior replacement worker. In addition, the university has a clinical instructor who has current experience in schools, which supports closer ties between the university and schools. There are also benefits for the school district, including professional development opportunities for Casey and access to the best and brightest of a college of education's new group of graduates, who can act as her replacement. When these arrangements work out, as they did in Casey's situation, they may continue for many years.

Initially, lecturers would seem to be a good pool from which to draw university supervisors. The lecturer on leave from a teaching position would seem to be an especially good choice, since this individual was handpicked and knows local schools. At the same time, even lecturers pose challenges. Whether they be clinicians like Casey or not, they often have heavy teaching loads, and there is a compounding difficulty in that the employment arrangement is so specialized that there simply are not a lot of instructors in this category. Finally, regardless of the type of lecturer, lecturer positions tend to be renewed annually, which does not support the development of university supervisors over time.

Having methods instructors such as Doug serve as a university supervisor creates the possibility of a powerful learning experience for both the preservice teacher and the faculty member. Having a faculty member follow the preservice teacher into the field allows the preservice teacher to receive immediate feedback on his or her campus assignments in the field setting, and the methods instructor can determine whether students correctly understand the assignments in a particular course. Despite these benefits, there are also challenges. Unlike Doug, many methods faculty may not have taught school in years, or even decades, and placing them in schools can challenge their skills. Methods faculty have also undertaken significant specializations in their advanced studies and are not necessarily able to meet the needs of preservice teachers equally. For example, Doug has specialized science knowledge but lacks specialized knowledge in mathematics, the second subject area being taught by the preservice teachers he supervises. Further, methods faculty often already have significant advising and credentialing responsibilities that exceed those of foundations faculty, and having these faculty drive to remote school sites can limit the time they have to develop their academic scholarship. With the potential of fewer academic publications and grants, it is not hard to see why methods faculty with heavy field responsibilities can be marginalized from peers who spend less—if they spend any—time in the field.

*A Single Model with a Range of Cooperating Teachers.* Like university supervisors, cooperating teachers have a wide range of experience. Some cooperating teachers have less experience in teaching and some have more; some have less university course work and others more; some have taken less leadership in their school and others more; some have drill-based instructional techniques and others are more experiential or inquiry based; some have limited mentoring skills and others more; and some have the knowledge and skills to meet the needs of their students in a minimal way and others more. At first glance it would seem to make sense that the university observe the cooperating teacher to determine the quality of the placement, but for an outside agency to evaluate an employee of a school would obviously be extremely problematic.

For this reason and others, a typical approach is that the college of education announces minimum requirements. Cooperating teachers involved in middle-level field experiences, for example, might need to be licensed in their content and have completed 2 years of teaching. Cooperating teachers hosting student teachers, on the other hand, might need additional years of teaching experience and to have previously hosted a preservice teacher in their classroom.

One challenge posed by announcing only minimal requirements is that the knowledge base and skills of the cooperating teacher are not well known to the university. In the triad model the teaching competency of the cooperating teacher is undetermined, so teacher educators do not know whether a preservice teacher can observe quality modeling of teaching. Cooperating teachers also receive little or no training in supervision, and so they may not understand how to best help a preservice teacher. Although they may be expert teachers, they may be horrible mentors. Indeed, many experienced teacher educators can name at least one cooperating teacher who has said to a student teacher on the latter's first day of student teaching, "It's sink-or-swim time: Here are the keys. If you have any problems I am in the teacher's lounge."

Readers should not take from these caveats that all cooperating teachers cannot teach and cannot mentor. Many cooperating teachers are accomplished teachers with advanced degrees in supervision or curriculum. The point is that in the traditional triad, there is no sophisticated mechanism to address differences in a cooperating teacher's knowledge, skills, and dispositions in teaching or his or her ability to supervise beginning teachers. In a redesigned model, relationships could be customized to support quality learning experiences for all participants.

***A Single Model with a Range of Preservice Teachers in a Range of School Sites.*** While it is true that the teaching force is composed of a narrow demographic (Darling-Hammond & Sclan, 1996), like many teacher educators Demetria has found that the students she places bring a wide diversity of life and professional experiences to their studies. Not only do these preservice teachers have varied backgrounds, but they also have a wide range of ability in their ability to teach. Despite what they may have learned in their campus classes, some seem gifted at teaching but are challenged at exit exams. Others are intellectually bright but have lessons that are disorganized and that do not support student learning. Still others are the whole package: preservice teachers who excel both at their content area academic courses and their education courses and who have the ability to put that knowledge to use in a classroom by planning and leading brilliant lessons that lead to student learning and growth. Despite this range of background and initial ability, in a typical triad model all preservice teachers are supervised in the same way.

Another limitation of the traditional supervision model is that it does not support the special needs of rural or urban schools, both of which have high needs for teachers. In rural areas, for example, there are a limited number of school sites where a preservice teacher can be placed. Since many rural schools only have one physical education or theater teacher for the district, the geographic area in which to place a college class of these teachers can be quite large. Regardless of the distance, teacher educators sometimes address these issues by simply sending the university supervisors on longer drives. Eventually schools become so remote that there is no way a supervisor could drive to them, so colleges of education simply do not use these schools, even though the schools often have high needs in terms of recruiting new teachers.

We also learned from Demetria's example that there are some urban contexts in which teacher educators will not place preservice teachers, because the schools are perceived as offering poor models of classroom instruction. These are the very same areas that have such high needs for teachers that city schools or districts will hire uncredentialed teachers with the requirement that those teachers complete their teaching credential on the job. In these cases, uncredentialed teachers use their own classrooms as the site for student teaching, and the experience is supervised by cooperating teachers who are likely to be colleagues of the uncredentialed teachers working in adjacent classrooms. Into this mix enters a university supervisor who may have limited understanding of working with these emergency credentialed teachers.

Teacher educators know that field experiences generally—and student teaching specifically—can be the most powerful experiences a preservice teacher can have in his or her teacher preparation program (Reiman & Thies-Sprinthall, 1998). Participants involved in supervision—whether they be preservice teachers, university supervisors, or cooperating teachers—bring a range of experiences, knowledge, skills, and dispositions to the field. Although each preservice teacher has unique needs, and although education reforms generally call for increasingly customized learning experiences, the one-size-fits-all model inherent in the supervision triad limits innovation and optimization.

## PLAN FOR THE BOOK

The contributors to this book propose alternatives to the traditional supervision model. This chapter proposed that a redesign of the traditional supervision structure might help address the limitations posed by a traditional approach. In the next chapter we share what others have learned.

In Chapters 3, 4, and 5, we offer three alternative models to the traditional triad. These models have been tested by teacher educator research teams at three different sites around the United States. The authors report what they have learned from their studies and offer important caveats for other teacher educators who may want to employ their methods.

These caveats or limitations suggest that a new model that has a *different structure* from that of the supervision triad could have many advantages. By "different structure," we mean that the use of three individuals— preservice teacher, cooperating teacher, and university supervisor—could be abandoned. Instead, supervision models might use specially trained and carefully selected cooperating teachers who might undertake the traditional functions of both a cooperating teacher and a university supervisor. In this alternative structure, cooperating teachers might work in pairs or groups. Likewise, university faculty could also be specially selected because of supervision skill, and they would be able to offer university classes on site at schools to both preservice teachers and cooperating teachers. In this way university faculty could disseminate and implement knowledge in multiple ways rather than just by working with one preservice teacher at a time. In this option, even preservice teachers might work in pairs or even clusters, perhaps learning to teach in many different classrooms and taking the best of what each cooperating teacher has to offer.

Finally, in this option, colleges of education would seize on the alternative structure to implement close partnerships with schools and to capitalize on the best of what each individual could contribute to the induction of preservice teachers into the profession.

In Chapters 6 and 7, the three alternative supervision models are compared, and we review how they inform the work of teacher educators. The challenges of implementation are also considered, with an emphasis on the benefits and challenges of the alternatives and the issues that remain to be addressed.

This book takes primary research and extends it by placing the research in the context of a redesign effort, as well as by reporting new information about the longevity of the alternative arrangements and new challenges posed by the alternatives. No claim is made that the traditional model of supervision should be abandoned in favor of alternative models. Indeed, the challenges posed by supervision are much more nuanced than to suggest that one model can be simply replaced with another. Instead, the three alternative supervision models described here are offered as a vision of what teacher educators could attempt as a part of future redesign efforts.

If readers were to implement one or more of these alternatives—or adaptations of them—then what works best and why in particular settings might be better understood. Through these redesign efforts, different supervision structures could be matched to particular school and personnel settings to support a rich and robust understanding of learning and teaching by all involved.

In traditional supervision models, classroom teachers serve as cooperating teachers or, if they are promoted to a leadership role, leave the classroom. In alternative supervision models, cooperating teachers could take leadership by being empowered in new roles within the classroom. In this way, supervision can be a vehicle for renewal that is initiated by the university because it promotes a structural change for supervisors. Such systemic change complements the local work led by the cooperating teacher and the university supervisor with the hope that it will lead to a ripple effect in redesigning the way schools and colleges of education can work together.

# PART I

# Background of the Challenges to Current Supervision Practices

# CHAPTER 2

# Attempts to Renew Traditional Supervision

*Deborah Bainer Jenkins and Cheryl Fortman*

THERE IS NO denying the significance of the student teaching experience to preservice teachers. When, as novice professionals, they are expected to understand teaching and learning, to take initiative, and to demonstrate competence in teaching skills, they draw more from their field experiences than from university coursework (Koerner, Rust, & Baumgartner, 2002). In one study (American Association of Colleges for Teacher Education, 1991), 75% of university supervisors and 70% of cooperating teachers agreed that student teaching prepares preservice teachers more than adequately for their first full-time teaching jobs.

The field experience itself, however, does not transform student teachers into skilled professionals. A review of research suggests that developing teaching skills is less a result of practice or field experience than a result of instruction and intervention (Gleissman, 1984). It is the experience itself and the practice of teaching skills within the experience that must be crafted by modeling, feedback, and reinforcement by competent supervisors. Thus, every member of the triad is important to the emergence of a new teacher.

We contend, however, that in today's educational settings the traditional triad model of supervision is, in the words of Mosher and Purpel (1972), "at best ineffectual and at worst a harmful form of interference" (p. 2) with the student teacher's development. After studying education schools, Levine (2006) concluded that there is no such thing as a typical program. He described teacher preparation programs as "unruly and disordered" (p. 109) and clinging to an outdated vision and strategy for educating teachers. He recommended that education schools transform themselves from ivory towers into professional schools focused on preparing basic practitioners adept at classroom practice—and doing so with pride.

The variation experienced by preservice teachers in various programs may be most evident during the student teaching or internship experience. Because of the lack of clarity in defining the roles and responsibilities of the members of the traditional triad, there is wide variation in the way cooperating teachers, university supervisors, and student teachers interact and, consequently, in the quality of the student teaching experience (Ganser, 1996). In addition, the incongruence between the practices and expectations of the university faculty, supervisors, and cooperating teachers reinforces the pressing need to redesign the present triad model of student teacher supervision. We propose that while the triad model may have been effective historically as a vehicle for the supervision and development of prospective teachers, it is not effective in the reality of today's educational context. The triad model is fraught with structural limitations that prevent it from being a workable model in current educational systems.

## LIMITATIONS OF THE TRADITIONAL TRIAD MODEL

Since the 1980s, prominent educators have called for reform and the simultaneous restructuring of K–12 schools and teacher preparation programs (Carnegie Task Force on Teaching as a Profession, 1986; Holmes Group, 1990; National Commission on Teaching for America's Future, 1996). Because they must be more responsive to their context, the transformation of K–12 schools is outpacing reform in schools of education, especially in teacher preparation programs. Sergiovanni and Starratt (2007) traced the evolution of supervision in schools, with an eye toward enhancing teaching, from a largely ritualistic event in the 1970s that used checklists as measures and actually did not matter very much through to a renaissance in the 1980s, during which clinical and artistic strategies for supervision emerged. By the mid-1990s, the focus changed from evaluating teachers to providing instructional leadership that promoted teacher development and built community among teachers, thus requiring supervisors to assume many new roles. The advent of the standards movement and the emphasis on curriculum in the late 1990s forced attention toward accountability. Teacher quality again took center stage and teacher professional development was reinvented from a series of isolated and often disconnected events to a unified, focused classroom-based commitment to continual development and improvement. Today, supervision in schools has morphed into a key function in the operation of schools driven by "cooperative leadership" (Wiles & Bondi, 2004, p. 97), although the nature and impact of these new supervision roles are still unclear.

While the purpose, roles, and processes of supervision in schools have changed drastically in the past 4 decades, the triad model of supervision applied to preservice teacher preparation has remained virtually unaltered. This triad model has been a part of university-based teacher preparation since the inclusion of the cooperating teacher in required field experiences in John Dewey's lab or university schools at the turn of the century (Tanner, 1997). Our experience suggests that the triad model, which implies equal responsibility and equal power within the unit, does not work in reality. When applied in most education programs, responsibility and power are not equal within the triad, and these relationships are often undefined, limiting the effectiveness of what could be a powerful supervisory partnership.

## Cooperating Teachers in the Traditional Triad

Koerner et al. (2002) explain that cooperating teachers establish the intellectual and affective tone for the experience and determine what the preservice student will learn. Cooperating teachers are in a unique position to help field experience students adjust to the school context, develop a place among the faculty, acquire materials, and explore the multidimensionality of teaching by involving them in instructional planning and evaluation, observing and analyzing their teaching, and providing feedback and reinforcement. Cooperating teachers are especially important when they are working with student teachers. They are able to provide immediate feedback and modeling and to help student teachers explore their instructional decision making and thinking about teaching. It is no wonder that student teachers rate the influence of the cooperating teacher as the highest among that of others of significance when it comes to personal support, role development, and professional skills (Copas, 1984). The importance of the cooperating teacher is underscored by the fact that traditional instruments that evaluate student teachers focus on how much these preservice teachers have learned about teaching, not on what was learned and transferred from university classes (Anderson & Radencich, 2001). Thus, the quality of the student teaching experience and the level of teaching skill attained by the student largely depend on the quality of the cooperating teacher and the classroom (Copas, 1984). Yet there is little research on what makes a good student teaching placement or a good cooperating teacher (Koerner et al., 2002).

Some educators express concern about the influential role of the cooperating teacher, suggesting that student teachers closely model the behavior of their cooperating teacher instead of exploring the theoretical and general principles that would enable them to translate their teaching skills into a variety of classroom situations. In 1904, John Dewey cautioned that student teachers' close contact with cooperating teachers may actually prevent them from developing the reflective thinking skills that enable them to analyze their own teaching and to make adjustments to different groups of students in educational settings (cited in Zahorik, 1988). While student teachers need cooperating teachers who are exemplary models of instructional effectiveness, they also must learn to become independent thinkers who explore the depths of classroom context and who can develop new techniques as needed. The supervisory role is critical to leading student teachers into and through this reflective process.

Although the period of student teaching is a highly impressionable one for preservice teachers, cooperating teachers are generally ill prepared for this responsibility. While they may be comfortable guiding student teachers through day-to-day classroom events, they receive little, if any, training in how to lead student teachers beyond these events to analyze and reflect on their teaching and the profession. Often they hold unrealistic expectations of what the student teacher can or should do. Many are tentative about giving specific feedback about teaching performance or instructional decision making, especially if they suspect that the student teacher will be hurt or disappointed. While cooperating teachers have the opportunity to observe and provide immediate feedback to student teachers, they often use that time to work with small groups of students or to catch up on paperwork instead of carefully observing and commenting (Anderson & Radencich, 2001).

For the triad model to be effective, then, the quality of cooperating teachers must be ensured. Koerner and associates (2002) suggested that cooperating teachers should be selected not because of their willingness to work with a student teacher, but because they have the potential to be mentors. They recommend selecting cooperating teachers who are:

- Skilled at instruction and management
- Sensitive to the views of others through caring, active listening
- Accomplished and willing to articulate their craft and the nuances of school culture
- Supportive of student teachers by helping them analyze and reflect on their experience and to gain insights that will develop instructional skills
- Capable agents of change who can establish collaboration and a culture of professional development

But even with highly qualified cooperating teachers, the triad model is plagued by discontinuity, which limits the growth potential of student teachers. On one level, there is a lack of substantive communication and collaboration between cooperating teachers and the university. Because of this disconnect, a number of things are not clearly communicated: the goals and expectations for the student teacher, the preferred instructional approaches, or the policies and processes that frame the student teaching experience. In this context, the university supervisor and cooperating teacher misunderstand each other and too often lack unity in front of the student teacher. Without collaboration, the members of the triad continue to supervise and teach as they always have, instead of working as contributors to a supervisory team in a way that would enrich the triad.

On another level, the research literature shows that in many teacher preparation programs, there is little articulation between the academic course work and the practicum and no coherent philosophy of teaching and learning across the two worlds (Reiman & Thies-Sprinthall, 1998). Cooperating teachers see their primary task as initiating student teachers into the profession, but faculty members want them to be more analytical and reflective about instruction and to model critical instructional decision making rather than merely transmitting teaching practices from one generation of teachers to the next (Anderson & Radencich, 2001). While they recognize the time constraints experienced by university supervisors, many cooperating teachers are reluctant to assume this deeper supervision role because of their own time constraints; they see that as a job for the university supervisor, not for them.

John Dewey (1938) recognized this discontinuity in teacher preparation. More recently, Leavitt (1992) pinpointed sources of discontinuity in teacher preparation programs based on a worldwide study. Leavitt found that preservice teacher education is frequently guided by traditions, folklore, or fads rather than by consistent theory. He contended that this inconsistency across time and programs confuses undergraduates and leads them to value only real-world experience as the basis for their growth and development. Further, although we know that observing exemplary teaching strongly affects practice, Leavitt found that preservice teachers are exposed to relatively few outstanding teachers during their university coursework and field experiences. This lack of modeling limits both the repertoire of teaching behaviors that preservice teachers develop and their depth of understanding of the act of teaching. Teacher preparation is further complicated because we lack a knowledge base on how to work with preservice teachers as young adult learners. These factors are exacerbated, as Leavitt and others noted, by the lack of coordination between universities and schools regarding field experiences and the dearth of highly skilled teacher educators at universities and K–12 schools.

Recognizing that cooperating teachers are the keystone of the complex and important process of preparing teachers for excellence in classrooms, we support the rhetoric from prominent educators that training cooperating teachers to analyze their own teaching and supervisory techniques is one way to improve the effectiveness of the traditional triad. Half a century ago, Harvard president James B. Conant (1963) called for a new model for teacher preparation that mirrored the medical model of teaching hospitals by creating clinical teachers and clinical professors specifically prepared to educate, supervise, and develop future teachers. Building on their work in the 1950s, Goldhammer (1969) and Cogan (1973) responded to Conant's call and outlined a clinical supervision model that involved one-to-one, systematic, in-class observation and assistance for preservice teachers. Findings indicate that cooperating teachers trained as clinical supervisors become skilled at developmental supervision and grow in conceptual complexity and reasoning (Reiman & Thies-Sprinthall, 1998). Cogan (1973) admitted that wide-scale implementation of the clinical supervision model would require a large cadre of clinical teachers and supervisors and would not be cheap, but he contended that it would be cheaper than the costs associated with poor teaching, student failure, and teacher recruitment. But in spite of the promise it holds for teacher development, the intensive clinical supervision process has been seldom and poorly practiced over the years (Griffin, 1987).

About the same time, Mosher and Purpel (1972) defined clinical supervision as "planning for, observation, analysis, and treatment of the teacher's classroom performance" (p. 78). This view relied heavily on observational instruments that categorized verbal and nonverbal teacher-student interaction. This information could then be used as a framework for change and improvement of performance. Their model uses objective observation, analysis, and feedback and, when used to supervise teachers, allows for preconferencing with the university supervisor and later reflection by the teacher (for a helpful review of models developed in the late 1960s and early 1970s, see Acheson & Gall, 1987; Cogan, 1973; Goldhammer, 1969; and Kosmoski, 1997).

When teaching is viewed as various behaviors that can be observed and analyzed, a supervisor can use objective descriptions to help a preservice teacher study the behaviors of both the students and him- or herself. These behaviors can be recorded either by videotape or survey-type instruments and later analyzed by the preservice teacher or the supervisor. Flanders (1965) was one of the first researchers to develop a systemic way of observing teacher behavior and classroom verbal interaction, which, when adapted to classroom use, provides teachers information about their overt behavior in the classroom. Using the clinical model and an observation instrument, the university supervisor and the cooperating teacher, together or separately, can record classroom interaction and share that information with the preservice teacher, analyzing and giving suggestions for changes and improvements.

Another part of Conant's (1963) reform agenda calls for cooperating teachers and university supervisors to work collaboratively as equal partners in teacher preparation and in other projects that link schools and universities. As the relationship between schools and universities has evolved, variations of the traditional triad approach to supervision have peppered the literature on supervision, but most fall far short of the equality afforded in a true clinical supervision model. Universities have provided adjunct status to cooperating teachers that affords luxuries such as library privileges and preferred parking in exchange for cooperating teachers assuming fuller responsibilities, including awarding final grades and determining if student teachers are ready for certification. Cooperating teachers who are empowered with more responsibility in this way experience more professional growth, increase their self-confidence, and gain status among their colleagues, according to Wilson (1995). However, after participating in a more collaborative triad model, Zheng and Webb (2000) found that both cooperating teachers and university supervisors preferred more traditional roles, with cooperating teachers serving as mentors and with the university supervisors responsible for assessing, evaluating, and "delivering bad news" (p. 4). Calls for change in the way we prepare and supervise preservice teachers, it seems, are not always welcome.

Another model from the 1980s includes Glickman's (1981) developmental supervision. The supervisor meets and observes the teacher or preservice teacher and decides on which leadership style to use with that particular teacher—directive, collaborative, or nondirective. This model recognizes that teaching is very personal and that there are limits to quantitative measurement. However, the model is not often used with preservice teachers.

The supervision of teachers and preservice teachers has evolved from inspection and enforcement in the late 19th century, to scientific supervision in the early 20th century, to bureaucratic supervision to cooperative supervision, and to technical supervision by the mid-1950s. The move to an emphasis on curriculum began the change in supervisory practices, which included clinical and managerial supervision, and finally to cooperative leadership as seen today (Wiles & Bondi, 2004).

When these models are applied to student teaching, they include the triad of the university supervisor working with both the student teacher and the cooperating teacher. As a team, the traditional triad provides support for the student teacher and a collegial relationship between the university supervisor and the cooperating teacher. This triad model has been a part of university supervision since the inclusion of the cooperating teacher or mentor in required field experiences.

## University Supervisors in the Traditional Triad

The university supervisor is the least studied member of the traditional supervision triad, yet he or she plays a critical role in any field experience. Zimpher, deVoss, and Nott (1980) described university supervisors as watchdogs for the completion of university requirements during field experiences; facilitators of the relationships between students, cooperating teachers, and building administrators; and personal confidants for other members of the triad. Koerner and associates (2002) suggested that, in contrast to cooperating teachers, who are viewed foremost as teachers and role models and only secondarily as teacher educators, the university supervisor is viewed as a leader and mentor who can and should positively affect the field experience. Especially during student teaching, the university supervisor helps the preservice teacher make sense of the act of teaching in ways that will influence future practice. Most sources agree that the university supervisor is the primary liaison and communication link between the university and the school, yet little research explores the power and relational dynamics inherent in the complex interactions between the university supervisor, cooperating teacher, and student teacher. Notably, the university supervisor is the translator of the values and beliefs of the teacher preparation program, weaving program principals into the feedback provided to the student teacher and facilitating the transfer of theory and training from the university to the classroom (Anderson & Radencich, 2001).

Yet the value of the university supervisor in the supervision triad is often questioned. Some have suggested eliminating the university supervisor from the triad because of the comparatively low influence he or she actually has on the student teacher (Bowman, 1979; Zahorik, 1988). Wood (1989) stressed that the university supervisor is critical to the field experience but too often duplicates the cooperating teacher's role of observing and evaluating teaching. Instead, the university supervisor should function as a personal confidant to the cooperating teacher and student teacher (Zimpher et al., 1980) or manage the administrative, managerial, and technical aspects of supervision (Wood, 1989). Slick (1998b) found cooperating teachers who preferred little or no assistance from university supervisors; they wanted university supervisors to be available and accessible, but otherwise wanted the freedom and independence of supervising the student teachers themselves. These roles for the university supervisor position that person as an outsider and therefore an artificial addition to the student teaching experience (Bullough & Draper, 2004; Slick, 1998b).

This mixed bag of responsibilities for the university supervisor is further complicated by disagreement and lack of research on who should most appropriately serve in this role (Slick, 1998b). Too often, university supervisors are assigned on the basis of availability rather than experience, credentials, or skill sets (Koerner et al., 2002). University faculty members tend to have little time, energy, or interest in supervision or must justify the time they spend on supervision because of its impact on their other faculty responsibilities. Because most faculty members have not actively engaged with K–12 education for many years, many have become theoretically rather than practically oriented and focus on issues and concerns related more directly to their research (Slick, 1998b). Many university supervisors are retired teachers or principals employed as adjunct professors or graduate students, some with little or no teaching experience. Some university supervisors are trained in one supervision model or another; some learned to supervise through mentoring; others operate based on experience or memories of their own student teaching experience.

***Faculty Members as University Supervisors.*** Given the discontinuity characterizing teacher preparation programs, it seems logical that university faculty members would be the most appropriate university supervisors. Casey and Howson (1993) built a case for the importance of faculty members' involvement in supervision. They advocated that academics cannot develop sound educational theory in isolation from the field. Further, they pointed out that involvement with K–12 education is necessary if faculty members are to establish a basis for dialogue about teaching and learning with preservice teachers. In other words, faculty members need to be familiar with the challenges that students face in their field experiences in order to gain credibility in the classroom, to provide meaningful instruction, and to relate to the stress students feel related to their field experiences. Indeed, several educators (Casey & Howson, 1993; Winitzky, Stoddart, & O'Keefe, 1992) go so far as to suggest that all education faculty be required to be involved with field supervision and that they should be supported throughout.

We recognize that involvement of education faculty in supervision would enhance field experiences for preservice teachers, strengthen school-university partnerships, and improve teacher preparation programs in a number of ways. But in reality, education faculty members tend to provide lackluster supervision. When supervision is carried out by tenured or tenure-track faculty members, they often make the minimum number of visits needed to assign a practicum grade (Teitel, 1997). And as the hypothetical case in the previous chapter illustrated, there are reasons for this: Faculty members have teaching and other responsibilities on campus that limit the time they can spend in the schools supervising, observing, providing feedback, troubleshooting, and building partnerships (Anderson & Radencich, 2001; Teitel, 1997). Inefficient scheduling of field placements and the time required to travel to multiple sites increase the feeling that supervision takes too much time for the impact it makes or, worse yet, is a waste of time altogether. Further, preservice teacher supervision is not highly regarded or rewarded in the academy. Working with graduate students, conducting research, and publishing are the bases for merit pay, promotion, and tenure in most institutions now, so undergraduate work and supervision are a lower priority. Casey and Howson (1993) pointed out that fieldwork and action research conducted in schools is not given much weight for merit pay, promotion, and tenure. Faculty members heavily engaged in field-based research often have difficulty getting funding and approval for research for those agendas. Finally, some professors think they can have a greater impact through scholarship, research, and theorizing than by supervising field experience students (Teitel, 1997). From a fiscal point of view, they may be correct. In 1985, it was estimated that the cost of a university supervisor was $100 an hour to "conduct supervision that has little or no documented effect on student teacher behaviors" (Rickard, 1990, p. 86).

Our observations support these concerns with supervision performed by faculty members. Over the years, we have seen the gulf widen between faculty members doing supervision and those in other programs not so involved in the field at multiple institutions, comparable to what Casey and Howson (1993) noted. Even the professional development school movement (Darling-Hammond, 1999)—which seemed to hold so much promise as a vehicle for providing field-based teacher education, jointly planned and taught by university-based and school-based faculty—has largely been abandoned because faculty opted out, and the few who remained involved ran out of energy or did not make tenure (Winitzky et al., 1992). Those working as university supervisors tend to be regarded by university culture as second-class citizens and they have difficulty having their work recognized because it is considered soft on theory and lacking in rigor. Worse yet, supervision responsibilities tend to drift toward faculty members who are female, untenured, or both, thus of lower status in the faculty ranks.

**Adjunct Professors as University Supervisors.** Even fewer studies inform us about the experience of adjunct professors as university supervisors, although at many institutions they provide the bulk of the field supervision. Adjunct appointments are usually made to certified teachers who are not employed full time by school districts and who are interested in additional income, retired teachers or administrators who want to stay in touch with schools, and retired professors no matter what their specialty or how long it has been since they were involved with K–12 schooling. Adjunct professors are valued for their flexible time schedules, networks with area schools, and educational experience. In addition, they're cheap. Adjuncts are paid by the course, by the hour, or by the number of students they supervise without recognition of the substantial number of credit hours they generate. They are not paid benefits and generally don't require office space or academic support, making them a bargain, especially in tough budget times. They receive minimal training, if any, and are generally low maintenance. They do their work in a relatively stealthy manner, appearing on campus only when picking up or returning paperwork or for required meetings. Our experience has been that the quality of supervision provided by adjuncts varies widely, based on their past experience, professionalism, and commitment to the program and the profession.

In her case studies, Slick (1998b) noted the frustration that adjunct supervisors feel. One commented, "I think the university specializes in keeping you in the dark or they assume you know everything. It's the end of the semester, and I now have a handle on what I'm supposed to do" (p. 306). In short, the concerns expressed about cooperating teachers— lack of communication from the university, unclear roles, differing philosophies about good teaching and appropriate methods, lack of training in supervision skills—seem to apply equally to adjunct professors. Our own experience serving as adjunct supervisors for other departments or campuses echoes these frustrations, especially when challenges arise and you are without information about department policies or whom to contact for guidance. As Clark (2002) stated, supervisors of student teachers need more adequate compensation, but they also need the support and the time to connect, read, converse, and learn what it means to be a teacher educator rather than a "standardized, disconnected service provider" (p. 78).

***Graduate Students as University Supervisors.*** While the number of graduate students serving as university supervisors is great, especially at research universities, we know little about their experience. Slick (1998b) followed a classroom teacher into graduate school, where she served as a university supervisor. As a graduate student, she reported experiencing resentment from her public school colleagues and feeling like an outsider at the field site. As a classroom teacher, she had observed tensions and misconceptions between cooperating teachers and university supervisors that led to broken relationships, and she knew that many cooperating teachers have attitudes toward university educators. Similarly, she felt isolated from the university and longed for its support and direction. Applying organization theory, Slick (1998b) commented that when people change organizational roles, they see situations differently, requiring a shift in perspective. If that shift is not made, the individual feels like an outsider. Thus, university supervisors such as this graduate student often experience unresolved tensions and frustrations because they must juggle perspectives that characterize a variety of groups, yet they do not enjoy full membership in any of those groups. They are not classroom teachers, not fully graduate students, and not teacher educators. One graduate student described her experience as a university supervisor as "a new space and a new role that is being constantly negotiated" (Isik-Ercan, Kang, & Darling, 2006, p. 8), evidence of her effort to juggle multiple perspectives and roles.

The change in organizational roles and resulting tensions is especially pronounced with international graduate students who supervise field experiences. These supervisors often lack experience as students, student teachers, or teachers in the American educational system. Isik-Ercan (in Isik-Ercan et al., 2006) talked about her need to grasp the essentials of the K–12 school system and the university supervision system before she could begin to negotiate her roles and territory as a university supervisor with the cooperating teacher and student teacher. In that same paper, Kang noted that interpreting and understanding her role as a university supervisor was especially problematic when personal or relational problems emerged because of the cultural difference in how those situations would be negotiated. She sought out advice from experienced university supervisors so that she would not approach field problems solely on the basis of her personal experience and beliefs. Although uncertain about many aspects of supervision in American schools, these international students were able to define their territory and to create space for work that was meaningful and useful by serving as a negotiator between the cooperating teacher and the student teacher and by providing pedagogical help.

Our experience providing supervision as graduate students and subsequently working with graduate students as university supervisors supports the observations made by others (Isik-Ercan et al., 2006; Slick, 1998b). To work effectively in the traditional triad, graduate students need training in supervision. Being a veteran teacher or researcher does not provide the skills necessary for successful supervision. Graduate students need clear definition of the roles of each member of the triad, especially if they lack experience with American schooling and supervision. This is especially critical where teacher education programs provide multiple routes to certification because the dynamics and roles within the traditional triad vary across those certification models. Roles must be clearly operationalized, including differentiating the status, responsibility, and degree of decision making associated with each role. Finally, it is vital to ensure or bring about philosophical alignment within the triad, recognizing that those agreements are complicated by cultural differences derived from national, regional, ethnic, and gender differences.

## NEXT STEPS FOR THE TRADITIONAL TRIAD

After examining teacher preparation programs across the country, Levine (2006) concluded that "there is a real danger that if we do not clean up our own house, America's university-based teacher education programs will disappear" (p. 113). Indeed, it is our position that an important element in the delay in realizing teacher education reform and, relatedly, school reform is our continued commitment to a triad supervision model that is not working in today's context. We need a supervision culture and a cadre of prepared clinical educators and supervisors. Instead, we have discontinuity within teacher preparation programs and duplication of efforts within traditional supervision triads. To change teaching, we need focused conversation about general practice in teacher preparation, yet current practices reinforce and entrench a triad supervision model. Pushing beyond craft to professionalism will require a higher level of discussion about practice and a different kind of relationship with schools, beginning with field supervision.

# Three Alternatives to the Structure of Traditional Supervision

# Building to Strength: Paired Teaching and the Reconceptualization of Public School Practica

*Robert V. Bullough, Jr., M. Winston Egan, and Jeffery D. Nokes*

OVER THE PAST several years challenges associated with locating suffi-cient numbers of willing and qualified cooperating teachers to super-vise and mentor preservice teacher education students and student teachers have grown. Among these challenges, none has proved more knotty than that of needing to provide preservice teachers with greater opportunities to work with diverse student populations, especially because those diverse populations have dramatically increased. At the same time, accountabil-ity pressures are closing off access to such school placements for fear that turning over classrooms to novice teachers will negatively affect student learning and standardized test scores. Clearly, any solution to a problem as complex as this one requires a reconsideration of traditional approaches to teacher education practica not only to prevent harm to students but, potentially, also to increase student learning.

This is not the only reason for reconsidering traditional preservice edu-cation practicums, models of student teaching, and the associated approaches to supervision. Greater appreciation for the positive effects on teacher learn-ing of ongoing dialogue about teaching (Penlington, 2008)—such as the value of peer feedback and evaluation on student teacher learning (Hawkey, 1995) as well as increased recognition of the potential of teacher collaboration and team teaching to improve job satisfaction and performance (Margolis, 2008)— raise serious doubts about the wisdom of solo teaching as the dominant model of practice teaching. In the traditional solo model of practice teaching, su-pervisors or mentors provide a range of support for a single student teacher early during the experience. Over time they look to disengage from active involvement in the classroom as soon as possible to allow the beginner an opportunity to find his or her own way, including the development of a distinctive teaching style (Feiman-Nemser, 2001; Young, Bullough, Draper, Smith, & Erickson, 2005). Additionally, studies of the positive effects of mentoring on teacher retention (Ingersoll, 2001) and of peer coaching on teacher learning (Zwart, Wubbels, Bolhuis, & Bergen, 2008) attest to the importance of rethinking professional relationships to better support learning and to strengthen professional commitment. Howey and Zimpher (1999) make the point this way: "Most fundamental to the improvement of teacher education is addressing how all teachers are prepared to work with one another" (p. 294).

Each of these reasons played a part in convincing faculty members working within the teacher education program at Brigham Young University (BYU) to reconsider long-established approaches to practica, including the emphasis on solo teaching.

## THE CONTEXT

BYU is a large, private, religiously sponsored university. A founding member of the National Network for Educational Renewal (NNER) (Goodlad, 1994), BYU is primarily an undergraduate teaching institution. Admission is highly selective. Teacher education generally is understood to be a university-wide responsibility and commitment, and over many years the program has been large—enrolling roughly 500 preservice students a year—and labor intensive. As a member of the NNER, the university works closely with five local school districts educating approximately one third of the school-age children of the state in a far-reaching partnership. The partnership is supported by 14 clinical faculty and a slightly larger number of tenure-line faculty as well as numerous school-based associates who work directly with teacher education students and a center of pedagogy (the Center for the Improvement of Teacher Education and Schooling, housed at the university). The partnership is lead by a governing board composed of the five district superintendents, the dean of education, and the director of the center.

Membership in the NNER requires commitment to the simultaneous renewal of teaching and teacher education and to the Agenda for Education in a Democracy. As Goodlad and colleagues state:

> At the heart of the NNER [is] an effort to draw attention to the unique role of education in a democratic society and the need to foster sound educational policies and practices that would not only support the broad purposes of democratic schooling but would also make possible the ongoing process of renewal. (Goodlad, Mantel-Bromley, & Goodlad, 2004, p. 25)

One result of the partnership and the many renewal initiatives it supports (one being endorsement programs in mathematics and reading) and of commitment to the agenda is that preservice teachers and university faculty are usually welcomed into schools, and opportunities for interaction and for research are abundant and widely supported. Nevertheless, given the size of the program and the large number of students requiring field placement, coupled with an additional challenge of relatively high teacher turnover, establishing quality placements is a daunting task and a nagging problem. In a more positive vein, the commitment to simultaneous renewal and to the agenda encourages innovation, especially of practices that promote collaboration and professional learning consistent with democratic processes (Bullough & Baugh, 2008).

The elementary teacher education program is 3 semesters long. Field placements begin early and are continuous and of growing intensity, culminating in student teaching (a yearlong paid internship is also an option for select beginning teachers). The professional component of the secondary certification program also culminates in a semester of full-time practice teaching, but it includes fewer practicum experiences. All elementary and some secondary students are organized into cohorts (Bullough, Clark, Wentworth, & Hansen, 2001), which enables development of aspects of the shared ordeal advocated by Lortie (1975). One benefit of cohorts is that while students may not know one another well, they do have a shared experiential background useful for relationship building. In addition, the majority of students share a set of religious commitments emphasizing service and personal integrity.

## SUPERVISORY STRUCTURE

The Paired-Teaching Model (PTM) is deceptively simple. It involves placing two rather than one student teacher with a single cooperating or supervising teacher; in effect, the student teachers fully share one placement. At this stage in the development of the model, teacher education students in secondary social studies and mathematics and—depending on public school interest and support and university faculty commitment—in elementary education are given the opportunity to participate in the PTM or to solo teach. Potentially effective cooperating teachers do not always wish to work with two student teachers. The ramifications of the addition of a second teacher education student—of teaching with a partner—into a practicum setting are extensive. The PTM alters virtually every aspect of traditional solo practice: the roles and responsibilities of teacher education students and cooperating teachers, teacher-student relationships, time and curriculum organization, and school experiences of both teachers and students.

To this point, faculty responsible for teacher education and teacher education practicums have moved cautiously and deliberately while exploring alternatives to the traditional arrangement of solo teaching. No alterations have been made in university supervisor roles and responsibilities. Moreover, very little effort thus far has gone into developing special training for the participants in paired teaching, either cooperating teachers or preservice teachers. As interest in and commitment toward the PTM grow, we would expect this to be an important focus. Instead of committing additional up-front resources, a decision was made early in program development and testing to simply see what cooperating teachers and preservice teachers would do, how they would work and spend their time, and what they would accomplish, given the opportunity to work under altered conditions. In effect, we sought to determine the promise of the PTM in light of concerns about its sustainability over time, should additional resources be required. Hence, from the beginning of our exploration of the model, participants were given only an orientation to paired teaching and teacher collaboration and invited to participate in various studies of the new practice. Happily, many classroom teachers have been receptive to the idea; some are even anxious to participate, while others who were initially reluctant are now interested. Results from four studies will be reported in this chapter; they elaborate on the strengths, weaknesses, and apparent promise of altering teacher education practicums to emphasize teaching with a peer. When seeking themes, special attention was given to the costs and benefits for cooperating teachers, teacher education students, and school-age students.

## GOALS

As suggested, the goals of paired teaching are to alter the context of learning to teach and to supervise preservice teachers so as to take greater advantage of the potential synergies and benefits of teams. Another goal is to alter the support structure by including an additional beginning teacher in the mix. More specifically, drawing on extant research, the altered structure of student teaching is intended to:

- Reduce the number of low-quality student teaching placements and improve the quality of the remaining placements
- Increase student teacher and cooperating teacher learning by increasing the kind, quality, and amount of teacher interaction and reflection on teaching and the feedback given

- Encourage the disposition to invest in and support teacher learning and development through enhanced collaboration
- Enrich the quality of pupils' classroom experience and improve their learning
- Develop productive and satisfying relationships with students, as well as between participating teachers, both entry level and experienced

## DESCRIPTION: OUR STUDIES OF PAIRED TEACHING IN PRACTICE

This section briefly describes three published studies of paired teaching, the first two conducted in elementary schools and the third in secondary schools. Study results will be reported later.

"Rethinking Field Experience: Partnership Teaching Versus Single-Placement Teaching" (Bullough et al., 2002) involved gathering data from 18 elementary school cooperating teachers, 9 who worked with paired preservice teachers and 9 who worked with singly placed preservice teachers. Following an orientation to the university's teacher education program with which all the teachers were somewhat familiar and a description of the study to be conducted, volunteers were solicited to serve as cooperating teachers from two matched, urban, poor, and highly diverse schools. All placements were randomly made and involved the preservice teachers teaching Thursdays and Fridays for 13 weeks in anticipation of full-time student teaching. We gathered three types of data:

1. *Interviews.* Two interviews of the preservice teachers were conducted, one early and one late in the term, by a member of the research team. A set protocol was designed to reveal aspects of the cooperating teacher's and the beginning teacher's roles and relationships and teaming practices, how their decisions were made, and their assessment of the teaching experience. Cooperating teachers were also interviewed at the end of the term, and comparisons were made between the cooperating teacher's and the beginning teacher's understandings and experience.
2. *Time logs.* Preservice teachers kept daily logs of how they spent their time. These were then compared to determine differences between the singly and partner-placed preservice teachers.
3. *Audiotaping.* Two planning sessions were taped and transcribed for analysis. The intention here was to see if there were differences between the paired and singly placed preservice teachers in what was discussed and in how conversations proceeded.

A second study was planned to address some of the weaknesses of the first study. "Teaching with a Peer: A Comparison of Two Models of Student Teaching" (Bullough et al., 2003) was intended to be a fuller exploration and test of paired teaching, focusing on student teaching, rather than a preservice practicum. The general question guiding this study was "What are the benefits and possible shortcomings of paired, partnered student teaching as an alternative model of practice teaching?" More specifically, we sought to identify differences in the kind and quality of relationships that emerged between cooperating teachers and student teachers in the two models—solo teaching and paired, or partnership, teaching. We also analyzed the models to ascertain differences between them in roles; responsibilities; values; and impact, particularly on student learning. Like the first study, this one was conducted in a highly diverse urban elementary school where nearly half the students were classified as either non–English speaking or limited–English speaking. With a reliance again on volunteers, assignments were made randomly. Single-placed student teachers were assigned to teach second (two student teachers), third, and sixth grades. Paired student teachers taught second, fourth, and sixth grades. Hence, 10 student teachers participated in the study along with, initially, seven cooperating teachers. Cooperating teachers were told to develop their own way of working with the student teachers that made most sense to them and that would be of most benefit to the children and to the student teachers.

As with the first study, data for this study included use of time logs, audiotaped planning meetings, and interviews of all student teachers and cooperating teachers. In addition, a set of interview questions was developed to assess student attitudes toward having more than one student teacher. Focus groups from each of the paired student teacher–taught classes were conducted. To portray development over time, cases were written of each placement and a cross-case analysis conducted, with special attention given to outliers. The two cases judged most representative of the single and paired placements were presented, and then compared.

The third study shifted terrain, moving away from elementary school teaching and teacher education to secondary school teaching and teacher education. We studied how the cooperating teachers conceptualized their roles and responsibilities and how they affected learning outcomes, both positively and negatively. The intent of this study, "The Paired-Placement of Student Teachers: An Alternative to Traditional Placements in Secondary Schools" (Nokes, Bullough, Egan, Birrell, & Hansen, 2008), was to illuminate the nature of the relationships that emerged between pair-placed secondary student teachers, especially the degree to which these relationships in both lesson planning and instruction could be characterized as genuinely collaborative. Twenty-six volunteer social studies student teachers were assigned to student teach with a partner. Some members of these 13 teams knew one another, but most were not well acquainted. As with the other studies, cooperating teachers volunteered to participate and attended an orientation describing the planned changes in student teaching. Final placements were made on the basis of subject area fit and student teacher grade-level preferences. Seven of the 13 teams student taught in high schools, five in junior highs, and one in a middle school. Six teams paired a woman and a man, six teams paired women, and one team paired men. In addition to working with a cooperating teacher, each team of student teachers was supported by a university supervisor who observed weekly. In addition to working within the placement classrooms, in accordance with established practice, student teachers participated in a monthly seminar with their university supervisor that provided additional support as well as a safe place for expressing concerns and exploring issues.

Data sources included interviews of 23 of the 26 student teachers (three student teachers were unable to be interviewed) and seven of the mentor teachers (for various reasons, six mentor teachers were unavailable for interviewing). Conducted by a member of the research team who had no formal connection to the student teacher, interviews were audiotaped and transcribed for analysis. Reflecting the value of student interviews found in the second study, 29 randomly selected seventh-grade, ninth-grade, and high school students representing each respective placement site participated in one of five focus groups. Interviewers sought to reveal the strengths and weaknesses of paired teaching and the nature of the relationships that developed between paired student teachers and their cooperating teachers. Focus group questions were far ranging and designed to provide a sense of what the students thought about being taught by paired student teachers, the strengths and weaknesses of the PTM, and any problems or issues they had with this approach to teaching. On the basis of a set of rubrics for collaboration in planning and instructing, and following analysis of the data set, each team of teachers was placed on a 5-point scale, whose measures ranged from "fully independent" to "fully collaborative" in how they worked together. Because teams worked in different ways when planning lessons and when actually teaching, the use of two separate scales proved necessary and informative (see Figures 3.1 and 3.2). To illustrate patterns within the data, three cases were presented. One was an outlier, a pair of student teachers who neither planned together nor taught together. Two were representative of the dominant collaborative patterns of teaching and planning in the data.

As with the first two studies, no special training was offered to cooperating teachers in how best to facilitate student teacher collaboration. Again,

**Figure 3.1.** The number of teams placed on each location of the "Collaboration During Planning" continuum and the locations of the three teams described.

| Peter & Jenny | | | Rhonda & Melanie | Joan & Amber |
|---|---|---|---|---|
| ⇩ | | | ⇩ | ⇩ |
| 1 | 3 | 3 | 4 | 2 |
| Fully independent | Mostly independent | Minimally collaborative | Moderately collaborative | Fully collaborative |

our interest was to see what would be done by both student teachers and cooperating teachers when they were presented with an alternative structure to solo student teaching. We recognized that in contrast to elementary schools, secondary schools entail a very different set of learning opportunities. For example, elementary school faculties are commonly organized into relatively small grade-level teams that meet often and for a variety of reasons. In contrast, secondary school faculties are organized into subject area departments that often are very large and serve as the foundation of teacher identity and sense of belonging. Frequently attracted to teaching because of their disciplinary interests and desire to work independently and given the fragmented structure of the day, teaming in secondary schools is very rare.

A fourth study was conducted to respond to the concern of a few study participants who considered paired-teaching to be "unrealistic." This study will be described in a separate section.

**Figure 3.2.** The number of teams placed on each location of the "Collaboration During Instruction" continuum and the locations of the three teams described.

| Peter & Jenny | | Joan & Amber | Rhonda & Melanie | |
|---|---|---|---|---|
| ⇩ | | ⇩ | ⇩ | |
| 1 | 1 | 3 | 8 | 0 |
| Fully independent | Mostly independent | Minimally collaborative | Moderately collaborative | Fully collaborative |

## RESULTS OF THREE STUDIES

Results from the first three studies lead to several conclusions about paired placement of practicum students. Organized thematically, discussion of these conclusions follows.

### Curriculum and Instruction

Given that the preservice teachers in the first study were within the schools only 2 days a week, it was not surprising that they, like the single-placed teachers, worked within the curriculum structure set by the cooperating teacher. Cooperating teachers set the agenda for planning meetings for both singly and pair-placed preservice teachers in this study, but those agendas opened and broadened somewhat as the term progressed. Most especially, evidence suggests that the paired preservice teachers came to enjoy greater curricular control, while the single-placed student teachers strayed little from the set program of instruction established by the cooperating teachers. It appears that, in part, this difference was the result of cooperating teachers having a greater trust of the paired teachers—who spent 30% more time planning than their singly placed peers—as well as greater preservice teacher confidence.

The paired preservice teachers reported that the curriculum was richer, and the data suggest that there also was greater instructional variability. For example, compared with those of singly placed preservice teachers, paired teachers' students spent twice as much time working in small groups and $1/5$ less time in whole-group instruction. Not only did the students receive more assistance from the paired preservice teachers but, importantly, they interacted more with one another.

These findings were echoed in the second study but with an important difference: Given increased resources and highly able student teachers, there was evidence of extensive instructional and curricular innovation—of moving outside, and sometimes well beyond, established classroom practice. These innovations included, for example, development of an art-and-dance program and of new learning centers. This profoundly influenced the cooperating teachers' own views of teaching and learning as well as their role as cooperating teachers.

### Student Teacher Relationships

Some of the teams in the first study divided instructional time, but half characterized their work as being "full teaming," fully sharing every aspect of the classroom and of teaching. Virtually all the paired preservice

teachers in this study liked working with a partner; and when compared
with their singly placed peers, they expressed greater confidence about
teaching and overall were more positive about the practicum experience.
Paired preservice teachers generally gave one another a great deal of social and emotional support, provided feedback on specific lessons, shared
ideas and insights useful for planning, served as aides while partners assumed responsibility for classroom instruction, and helped with classroom
discipline. Bonnie, a preservice teacher from this study, nicely captured
the nature of the paired preservice teachers' experience:

> When there's two of us, I really feel like you can talk, and pat each
> other on the back and lift each other up. Yes, you can get that from
> your mentor teacher, but sometimes they don't understand how
> serious we're taking [teaching] in our hearts.

In addition to feeling well supported, they worried less and thought their
classroom management was better. This was a point supported by analysis of the planning tapes where classroom discipline and management were
seldom discussed, and paired preservice teachers became invested in one
another's learning and growth. In contrast, the singly placed preservice
teachers felt rather disconnected, not well supported by their cooperating
teachers, whom they recognized as being very busy people, lonely, and
very concerned about classroom discipline and management.

Remarkably, we found no evidence of feelings of competition between
student teachers in any of the studies, which suggests that all felt comfortable with their emerging performance as teachers; they all had abundant opportunities to grow and to learn together, and they felt they were
positively contributing to the learning of their students. Yet, as Walsh and
Elmslie (2005) suggest, competition between team members remains a
potentially serious issue that especially complicates the difficulty for cooperating teachers and university supervisors of giving feedback on teaching that is fair—avoiding comparison—as well as useful and helpful.

## Cooperating Teacher Roles and Relationships

Across the three studies, cooperating teachers reported that they enjoyed
observing the preservice teachers teach; doing so gave them additional
insights into the students in their classes and sometimes they learned something new. Teachers in the first two studies valued having an "extra pair
of hands" in the classroom, allowing them sometimes to work with a student individually if warranted. As they witnessed the pairs planning and
teaching, they came to hold greater levels of trust and confidence in the

preservice teachers than did cooperating teachers working with a single preservice teacher. Some chose to become team members rather than stay on the fringes of classroom activity. Recognizing that the preservice teachers usually went to one another for support and feedback rather than coming to them, the cooperating teachers of paired elementary teachers generally encouraged the trend, saying that this was a good way for beginners to learn about teaching and to solve problems.

Cooperating teachers proved extremely influential in each study, either opening or closing opportunities for collaboration. Nearly all the secondary school cooperating teachers in the third study, for example, insisted on a mix of solo teaching and team teaching. Thus, one team, judged "moderately collaborative" in both planning and instruction, was paired for five classes while soloing in a single class. One unfortunate result of this arrangement was that these student teachers did not share a planning period. During classes they tag teamed (as they described their actions), taking turns teaching sections of a lesson for which they accepted responsibility rather than fully sharing the classroom. Finding time to meet together to plan proved very difficult for this pair.

When asked about the drawbacks of supervising two preservice teachers, the elementary cooperating teachers commented that initially working with two was more stressful and time consuming than working with one. Yet almost all concluded that whatever additional time was required was worth the investment because, among other reasons, "they bring wonderful things to the classroom!" Of special note, the teachers said that the energy level in the classroom had increased with two preservice teachers at work, individual school-age students received additional and needed assistance, and the curriculum had been enriched. Giving feedback to two rather than one preservice teacher was time consuming for cooperating teachers, but the paired preservice teachers' reliance on each other for support lowered the expectation and need for feedback from their mentor. Not surprisingly, a few noted that the power relations were altered in the classroom and that they changed traditional cooperating teacher roles and interactional patterns. Rather than disengage from the classroom, most of the cooperating teachers of the paired preservice teachers actually remained involved, and they took advantage of the opportunity to become part of the team. The implication here is that the cooperating teachers began to reconsider the nature of their work. Speaking of the effects on school-age students of paired teaching, one cooperating teacher succinctly expressed the general view of her colleagues: "Two are a lot harder than one. . . . There is more preparation time, [it] requires more feedback, but it is worth it because it is better for the children to have two [teachers]." This teacher said that she hoped in the future she would have paired student teachers.

In particular, the paired model of student teaching transformed how cooperating teachers who participated in the second elementary study thought about and performed their roles and responsibilities. As noted, in solo student teaching, as was true in this study, student teachers often are charged with carrying out the cooperating teachers' program of instruction and then at some point are left alone to make their own way with relatively little support. In contrast, the paired student teachers and their cooperating teachers had a very different experience and relationship, although in varying degrees. Dialogue about teaching was constant, consistent, and more conversational and less one directional than supervisory as peers planned together and observed one another teach. Under such conditions, both the cooperating teachers and the student teachers asked for and received feedback—which was often critical—on their teaching. Unlike what they experienced in supervising singly placed student teachers, cooperating teachers found it relatively easy to turn over increased responsibilities early to the student teachers and to encourage risk taking and curricular experimentation. Trust grew quickly and cooperating teachers easily slipped into supportive roles, often choosing to work on the sidelines with individual students or sometimes in a small group. The elementary cooperating teachers tended not to disengage fully, but rather stayed involved, seeking to add to the quality of the pupils' learning experiences while not distracting from the student teachers' responsibilities or authority. The cooperating teachers reported that one reason to stay engaged was that the curriculum was much enriched. Lessons were varied and interesting and better for children.

## Model Value and Pupil Learning

Each of the paired student teachers in the first two studies found the experience valuable, although one in the first study said she would have preferred being placed alone. In contrast to her peers, Rachel concluded that paired teaching was not "realistic." This statement presents a serious issue, as Kahne and Westheimer (2000) observe: "The need to free prospective teachers to develop powerful educational visions and to imagine new possibilities, although important, may come into conflict with the need to prepare them for schools as they currently exist" (p. 380). Nevertheless, the data across all four studies examined in this chapter strongly support the value of paired over solo student teaching: "Having a partner who was also a peer opened up opportunities for development unavailable to single-placed student teachers and had the additional value of enabling risk taking both singly—where the boundaries of one's autonomy are pushed outward—and unitedly" (Bullough et al., 2003, p. 68).

As is common among cooperating teachers generally, those participating in these studies, both those working with singly and paired-placed student teachers, found value in their experience. However, evidence was found of some rather unique influences. For example, in the second study, the cooperating teachers, who, as is commonly reported, had been concerned that allowing student teachers into their classrooms would negatively affect student learning, said that the children actually learned more and learned more quickly than before. In the focus groups, the children consistently echoed their teachers' assessments, claiming that they liked having two student teachers in the classroom and believing that they were learning more.

**Concerns**

Cooperating teachers in the second study thought that once the paired student teachers left the classroom, their students would have some difficulty transitioning back to the way things had been before their arrival and that their students had got used to receiving more attention and assistance than could be provided by one teacher—even an experienced and skilled one—alone. Additionally, they said that they would miss interacting with the student teachers and that they enjoyed working closely with other teachers. The one genuinely negative concern that was identified (and results were mixed on this point), and a concern also noted by Walsh and Elmslie (2005), was that paired teaching might be more labor intensive for cooperating teachers—especially, we suspect, where a team fails to gel productively. This possibility remains a concern but ironically it arose twice in the single teaching placements between student teachers and their cooperating teachers and not between student teachers in the paired placements. Here it is worth noting the conclusion drawn by Baker and Milner (2006) in their study of paired teaching: "The most significant finding of our study, we argue, is that paired student teachers learned more from mentor teachers than did students who taught alone" (p. 66). A conclusion such as this suggests that the additional effort is likely worthwhile, especially when increased student learning also results.

In the secondary school study, mention was made by a few pupils that they had difficulty building relationships with two teachers. Some of the student teachers commented that finding time to plan together was extremely difficult. In contrast to their previous experience with student teachers, cooperating teachers of the secondary school student teachers reported being less involved with paired beginning student teachers, often discovering that they were the last resort after student teachers had tried to resolve problems on their own. In effect, and as noted previously, the power structure shifted dramatically, and in some respects the resulting change in role appears to have been a bit uncomfortable for a few of the secondary school cooperating teachers. At the same time, several of the secondary cooperating teachers reported that they were called upon to perform a new function as mediator. For all but one of these cooperating teachers who were asked to mediate differences between student teachers, this presented rich learning opportunities: "Some mentor teachers were instrumental in helping team members work through periods of disagreement and tension, encouraging student teachers to reflect on disagreements and reach a compromise" (Nokes et al., 2008, p. 2174).

Clearly, in contrast to working in a paired placement within an elementary school setting where the norms of teaming are more common, we found the secondary school setting provides an easy escape. Organization of the school day into discrete classes and time periods meant that rather than confronting problems associated with learning to team, at the first sign of tension separate assignments could be made that allowed for soloing. Thus, the one team (the outlier in the third study) was split almost immediately by the cooperating teacher, who later admitted that he did not like the idea of paired teaching, because, as he said, "'I never had that experience and they're never going to have it [again] if they get a job [teaching]. I just don't think that's fair to them'" (Nokes et al., 2008, p. 2171). Why this cooperating teacher volunteered for the study is uncertain; and no answer was forthcoming. These two student teachers, while admitting that their styles were very different, divided their cooperating teacher's teaching assignment and solo taught, never really having had the opportunity to begin to work through their differences.

In varying degrees, each pair of student teachers in each study confronted the challenge of working through their differences in views and approaches to teaching and content area understanding. This issue again proved most vexing for participants in the third study, involving secondary education teaching. For the outlier pair in this study, under the influence of their cooperating teacher, such differences were judged a liability. Supported by their cooperating teachers, other teams, including those working in elementary schools, thought of such differences as assets, noting, as one remarked, that "ideas double or even triple because there are two of you up there with different points of view" (Nokes et al., 2008, p. 2172). While tension is inevitable in teaming, most teams moved toward compromise and increased understanding, with the result that a richer and more interesting curriculum emerged. Comments made by pupils within the focus groups underscored this point: "It is kind of like you have two different opinions and you can . . . form your own opinion based on the two" (p. 2172).

## NOT A "REALISTIC" EXPERIENCE: A FOURTH STUDY

We wanted to see if, or in what ways, teacher education students who had been placed in pairs for student teaching were advantaged or disadvantaged as 1st-year teachers. Were the few study participants who asserted that paired teaching is not realistic correct? In "Teaching with a Peer: A Follow-up Study of the 1st Year of Teaching" (Birrell & Bullough, 2005), visits were made to the schools of eight 1st-year teachers who had student taught with a partner. Three of these teachers obtained positions in inner-city schools in three different states; one taught in a depressed farming area near St. Louis, Missouri; another in Northern California in a majority Hispanic elementary school; and three at suburban schools. The schools varied dramatically in size, age, and student body composition. Data included classroom observations and interviews with the beginning teachers; their school principals; and, where possible, their assigned mentors.

Seven of the eight beginning teachers who participated in the fourth study of 1st-year teachers told a remarkably similar story. These seven teachers reported being well satisfied with their teacher preparation and mostly well prepared for teaching. Their principals (again with the single exception) thought they were exceptional beginning teachers. For instance, one said that she had "never seen anyone who's more collaborative, [who] can work more easily with an experienced team [of teachers]" Birrell & Bullough, 2005, p. 74). Another principal remarked of a second beginning teacher that she "admired her 'collegiality, her effective teaching,' and then said, 'I don't know if that's part of your model or the kids just come that way'" (p. 74). The seven teachers shared a view of the importance of collaboration in learning to teach well, even as they said they often did not have the amount, kind, or quality of professional interaction they hoped for. Yet they sought such interaction and feedback, generally not hesitating to ask for help when feeling the need for it. They liked having visitors, including parents, in their classrooms. From their experience, they thought it very important to get additional adults into the classroom because it increased opportunities to learn. Mentors also noted this desire for interaction, with one commenting, "'She bounces things [ideas] off people, runs things past them, and seeks feedback and input from others'" (p. 75).

The charge that paired teaching is unrealistic appears to be connected mostly to concerns about discipline and classroom management, such as whether a beginning teacher who had worked in a paired placement would be able to manage a classroom full of children on his or her own. Sharply focused on student learning, the principals and mentors were very positive in their reports of the beginning teachers' management skills. In addition, they noted that these teachers were unusually open to new ideas, in part because they appeared to have a clear sense of themselves as teachers and of their strengths and limitations:

> "[As a student teacher] I was within a safe environment. I was able to try out new things I wanted to do, experiment with my beliefs and ideas. I am still doing that. I bounce ideas off the people here. [But] it's not the same. [Still] I feel more confident. . . . [Paired student teaching] made me less afraid to ask for help." (in Birrell & Bullough, 2005, p. 77)

The eighth teacher presented a very different picture. Working in a rural area, which was undergoing dramatic changes, and facing a class of 27 fourth graders, this beginning teacher was assigned to a four-person instructional team composed of two other 1st-year teachers and one 2nd-year teacher. As the principal noted, there were problems within the team, which lacked leadership. The former student teacher's assigned mentor was little involved with her and of little assistance. This beginning teacher felt abandoned, and as she considered her student teaching, she remarked, "'I wish we had more time to teach'" (Birrell & Bullough, 2005, p. 79). She had not wanted to peer teach, but she did, and she thought the practice of little value. Describing herself as "reserved," and as preferring to "work alone," this beginning teacher concluded that she was not well prepared for her current teaching assignment.

Although it is impossible to make any direct or clear causal connections between paired student teaching and the performance or experience of these beginning teachers during their 1st year of teaching, the fact that one teacher encountered such difficulties while others thrived underscores a simple and perhaps obvious point: No approach to teacher preparation can possibly be fully adequate given the dramatic variations in work contexts, school cultures, biographies, and personalities of beginning teachers. There is no one best system of teacher education or practicum design.

## INFORMING CHANGE

Across the four studies, whenever the paired student teachers stayed engaged with one another, an especially rich, reflective learning environment was created within which they could learn about and practice teaching. Both student teachers and cooperating teachers noted that under such conditions, opportunities for giving and receiving feedback were constant and learning accelerated. Of special note, it is readily apparent that feedback on teaching given by a cooperating teacher is experienced quite differently from feedback offered by a peer. Cooperating teachers and university supervisors are charged with evaluation as well as facilitating teacher development, which may serve to limit dialogue and increase conformity. What is most needed by the student teachers is focused, ongoing, and critical but supportive conversations about teaching and learning to teach. With few exceptions, in each study the student teachers were judged by their cooperating teachers to be more confident than singly placed student teachers; the curriculum was richer and instruction more varied; and when pupils were interviewed, they reported learning more. Respecting this last point, in the focus groups conducted for the secondary school study pupils were aware that with two teachers they were more on task, and as one remarked, "'I have noticed that because there [are] two of them I have been paying attention more and I have been getting better test scores'" (Nokes et al., 2008, p. 2173).

One conclusion of importance for cooperating teachers drawn from the secondary school study and following from the others reported here bears special mention: "[Cooperating teachers] need to understand that their roles as a mentor of a pair of beginning teachers is fundamentally different than their role as the mentor of a solo student teacher" (p. 2174). Ironically, as the outlier pair in the secondary school study illustrates, placing two student teachers together is not a simple solution to the problem of insufficient numbers of quality teaching placements. Since the demands placed on cooperating teachers who work with paired student teachers are in some important respects different from those faced by cooperating teachers who work with single student teachers, direct attention needs to be given to helping cooperating teachers develop the requisite skills and understandings to be successful in what is a new assignment and learning opportunity. While the studies reported here indicate that even with relatively little special assistance or training, much good comes of paired placements for cooperating teachers, student teachers, and pupils, it is readily apparent that the next stage in our work is to develop a program of instruction and support to maximize the educative potential of the PTM. The rubrics—the scales—for collaboration in planning and instruction developed for the secondary school study offer a very promising point of departure for such work.

Even without emphasizing training in collaborative teaching practices, the studies offer strong evidence that the PTM model opens opportunities to learn about teaching and for development as a beginning teacher that are comparatively rare. By altering the nature of student teacher and cooperating teacher relations, it also provides fresh possibilities to help cooperating teachers to grow and develop as mentors and as teachers. Importantly, the model shifts emphasis away from apprentice approaches to learning to teach, allowing both beginning teachers and their supervisors to think deeply and together about the problems and possibilities of teaching. As a scaffolded environment of the sort captured by Vygotsky's concept of the zone of proximal development (John-Steiner, 1978), paired teaching offers beginning teachers the temporary support needed to avoid being overwhelmed by the demands of teaching while learning to manage and resolve its challenges. Moreover, it strengthens the disposition and desire to work collaboratively with other educators, a key to long-term professional growth and to school improvement.

Across the studies, evidence of scaffolding is abundant. For example, it was common for one student teacher to directly manage the discipline problems of the class while the other conducted whole-class instructional activities. These roles would be reversed on other occasions, so both student teachers gained experience in working with discipline issues; both would gain experience conducting whole-class activities, knowing that if something went awry, they would receive assistance—they would not have to engage in both types of activities simultaneously. Similarly, and especially in the elementary school settings, during periods of small-group or individual work, paired teachers and their cooperating teachers would often work together with students. This reduced the demands for attention placed on any one teacher while offering the opportunity to develop a greater knowledge of individual students and their educational needs. In the secondary school setting, the evaluation of student work, another unfamiliar and time-consuming task, was usually shared, with student teachers needing to come to agreement on rubrics and standards to ensure fairness. Thus student teachers gained experience in practical aspects of assessment without being overwhelmed by the amount of grading that was required.

Research on teacher learning supports the model of paired teaching for different reasons. Wilson and Berne (1999) suggested that effective teacher development requires "collaboration adequate to produce shared understanding, shared investment, thoughtful development, and a fair, rigorous test of selected ideas" (p. 175). They further claimed that dialogue that includes critique promotes teacher development, and this means tension—that differences in points of view are essential elements for teacher learning. With few exceptions, the paired student teachers in our studies experienced tension when one member of the team had ideas about teaching that did not match his or her partner's. Further, the studies suggest that having one's ideas challenged by a peer is different from having ideas challenged by a supervisor, and that difference is often positive:

> When differences in opinion arise between a mentor teacher and a student teacher it is much safer for a student teacher to disengage from the dialogue and yield to the mentor. However, when two student teachers disagree there

is an enhanced potential for rich interaction and reflection. (Nokes et al., 2008, p. 2173)

Through intense dialogue encouraged by sharing a classroom, a cooperating teacher, and experiences, the student teachers in our studies generally worked through their differences and learned as a result. As Bransford, Brown, and Cocking (2000) point out, coming to joint decisions requires teachers to "wrestle with issues" (p. 198). Clearly, dialogue is important to encouraging teacher development (Penlington, 2008).

An additional point about paired teaching and teacher reflection is that teaching is time-consuming and energy-intensive work, especially for inexperienced teachers and student teachers. The demands of planning, teaching, and assessing student work by oneself leaves little time or energy for reflection. Noting the opportunity his paired student teachers had to develop and reflect on their experiences of teaching, one of the cooperating teachers in the secondary study complained about his own student teaching, deciding that it had failed to measure up educationally.

We conclude with two questions: What are the optimal conditions for promoting the development and growth of entry-level teachers, particularly during the student teaching phase of preparation programs? Should the primary outcome of student teaching be surviving the experience, getting through the ordeal, or just getting along—just finishing the term? We think not. The positive outcomes for student teachers, their mentor teachers, and their school-age students reported here suggest that the paired placement of student teachers is certainly worthy of wider use and further study.

# CHAPTER 4

# Empowering Cooperating Teachers: Creating a Partnership to Support the Teacher Education Program

*C. J. Daane and Elizabeth K. Wilson*

THE CLINICAL MASTER TEACHER (CMT) alternative supervision model was established in 1991 at the University of Alabama (UA) as a result of faculty members seeking ways to strengthen our teacher education program by developing a model of collaboration with classroom teachers for the student teaching experience. In addition, faculty sought to develop this supervision partnership as a response to the cooperating teachers who perceived themselves to be in a subordinate role when participating in the traditional student teaching triad model. Our vision for the CMT model was to have teams of cooperating teachers in every school in our local area taking responsibility for student teaching supervision, evaluation, and assessment. We envisioned a partnership with these teachers that would help us strengthen our teacher education program through collaborative work based on combining research and practice.

## RATIONALE

The CMT model was built on research and reform (e.g., Carnegie Task Force, 1986; Holmes Group, 1990) that suggests the need to strengthen the preparation of new teachers through greater involvement of the classroom teacher. For our CMT model to work, experienced classroom teachers would need to be able to provide effective continuous constructive feedback to a student teacher without supervision by a university supervisor. This supervision would have to be at least as effective as the traditional triad model (student teacher, cooperating teacher, university supervisor) that was already in place.

According to Bowman (1979), the classroom teacher spends the most time with the student teacher and is in the best position to critique the student teacher's performance on a daily basis. We believed, moreover, that cooperating teachers, working together and so acting as a school team, would be able to provide extra supervision and assistance to one another.

The early hypotheses, at the inception of the CMT model, suggested that supervising a student teacher and assisting in the supervision of other student teachers in the school would help cooperating teachers view supervision from a broader perspective (Stanford, Banaszak, McClelland, Rountree, & Wilson, 1994). We had hoped that cooperating teachers who worked together within a school could benefit from their colleagues' experiences and expertise. Our expectation was that the teachers might begin to examine and change some of their own supervisory strategies. By collaborating with other teachers, the cooperating teachers could receive support for and validation of their efforts in supervision.

In addition to the benefits for the cooperating teachers, we considered the perspectives of the student teachers. It is the student teachers who often have felt conflicted in accepting the advice or direction of the cooperating teacher and the university supervisor, since these two people can view student teaching through different lenses (Guyton & McIntyre, 1990). In other cases, a coalition can be formed of the student teacher and the cooperating teacher, isolating the university supervisor. Veal and Rickard (1998) indicated that cooperating teachers and student teachers often bond together and establish a relationship that continues long after student teaching ends. In some earlier work, Elizabeth and a colleague suggested that there is little impact from the university supervisor on the student teacher's beliefs and practices (Wilson & Readence, 1993; see also Boydell, 1986).

We were prepared to embark on the development of the CMT initiative, knowing that there would be role changes for the university faculty and classroom teachers as well as conflicts that would have to be resolved for the partnership to work (Clift, Johnson, Holland, & Veal, 1992). University and school faculty found themselves involved in what Lemma, Ferrara, and Leone (1998) later described as "risk taking, problem solving, and troubleshooting" (p. 11), inherent components of forming a partnership between two entities. Players on both sides would have to begin to redefine their roles so a more egalitarian partnership could exist.

## CONTEXT

Historically, our teacher education programs in the Elementary and Secondary Teacher Education Programs at UA had been heavy on faculty involvement in clinical experiences, especially student teaching in which the traditional triad model had been in place. As faculty we prided ourselves on the positive interaction and communication we had with administrators and teachers working for local school systems. However, when the emphasis of the university began to shift more to research and less to service and teaching, faculty members found themselves with little time to be involved in clinical experiences. As faculty involvement lessened, we perceived a need to increase supervision of student teachers by other personnel. Outside supervisors were carefully selected; however, as student enrollment increased, there were not enough supervisors available who were familiar with UA teacher education programs. Thus, supervisors sometimes were used who had little knowledge of the pedagogy and content of current programs. Under the traditional supervision model, training for these supervisors consisted of a half-day meeting in which student teaching requirements were reviewed along with observation and evaluation forms, but with little or no explanation of previous course work taken by student teachers.

As the faculty began to withdraw from the supervision of student teachers, feedback at the end of the semester from cooperating teachers indicated some dissatisfaction. Teachers were beginning to question the value of some of the adjunct university supervisors and wanted more input into the observations and evaluations of their student teachers. The supervision model at that time allowed for 50% input from the cooperating teacher and 50% input from the university supervisor. However, it was the cooperating teachers who spent more time being involved with, providing feedback to, and mentoring the student teachers.

Research conducted after the implementation of the CMT model suggests that cooperating teachers rarely believe they have a valuable voice in the process of educating prospective teachers (Stanulis, 1995). They often view the university supervisor as an intruder who does not really understand the day-to-day operation of the classroom and who often becomes too authoritarian. C. J.'s research (Daane, 2000) on supervision added that cooperating teachers believe that they are the ones who really know the student teachers' abilities and are in the best position to do the supervision and evaluation. They want to feel empowered as professionals to observe, evaluate, critique, and help influence the next generation of teachers without obstruction from university supervisors.

Responding to the concerns of the cooperating teachers and the belief that a school-university partnership would contribute to a stronger student teacher experience for all involved, the faculty members in the Elementary and Secondary Teacher Education Programs began deliberating about ways to accomplish this. A review of the research suggested that experienced teachers could assume more responsibility for the supervision of student teachers in their classrooms and possibly replace the need for the university supervisor. Yates (1982) found that cooperating teachers probably have more influence on student teachers than do the college supervisor.

At first we were reluctant to release control of the supervisory aspect of student teaching, since this culminating experience has been shown to be the most influential one of the student teachers' initial licensure training. However, with the research recommending that teachers and university faculty come together to work as a team on problems facing teacher education, we decided to attempt to build a partnership for the purpose of improving student teaching supervision.

We knew that if this partnership was to be effective, both groups would have to have input and make joint decisions on how the partnership would evolve, function, and continually be evaluated for effectiveness. We also realized that our school-university partnership must establish mutual trust between all stakeholders. During the initial dialogue the responsibilities would have to be stated, the expectations outlined, and the realities addressed and discussed. As our fledgling partnership was starting to evolve, several elementary and secondary faculty members, along with two local classroom teachers who were serving as cooperating teachers, convened to establish the underlying premises for the creation of the school-university partnership in the area of student teacher supervision. Because these discussions began in response to an institutional shift in faculty responsibilities, the student teachers were not included in the initial planning for the CMT initiative.

During this initial planning, we realized that it would be necessary for the traditional triad model and the CMT model to be implemented concurrently and with similar requirements for the student teachers in our teacher education programs. The CMT initiative would begin with a small cadre of clinical master teachers with continual assessment of the model to determine if it would be viable for our teacher education programs.

## STRUCTURE OF THE CMT MODEL

The structure of the CMT alternative supervision model has continued to evolve from its inception in 1991. Faculty members interact with CMTs both formally and informally during the year to stimulate discussions on model revision and improvement. The original supervision model began with seven CMTs in 1991 and has expanded to include over 200 teachers in 42 schools. Clinical master teachers fulfill the traditional roles of both the campus-based supervisor and the school-based cooperating teacher, thus empowering the classroom teacher to take responsibility for the supervision and support of the student teacher. The CMTs are appointed as school-based adjunct faculty in the UA College of Education and receive $250 a semester for supervising a student teacher.

The ideal CMT model consists of a team of four to six teachers within one school, one student teacher per classroom teacher, and one university liaison. The CMT assumes responsibility for the assigned student teacher and provides continual and consistent feedback to and evaluation of the student teacher in conjunction with other team members.

The CMT team model may change slightly in a few schools because of factors beyond the control of the teacher education program. For example, if a school does not have four to six teachers, a team could exist with only two teachers. In any given semester there are 25–30 teams operating with a university liaison for each team. The liaisons—who are current faculty members, retired faculty members, retired classroom teachers, graduate assistants who have teacher certification, or classroom teachers who may be taking a leave of absence from their normal teaching assignments—can serve up to four teams each. If they are regular faculty members, serving three teams constitutes a course release. Two faculty members serve as coordinators of the CMT alternative (one at the elementary level and one at the secondary level).

## Selection of Clinical Master Teachers

Teachers who wish to participate in the model must submit an initial portfolio that includes details of their classroom teaching careers, their philosophy of teaching, letters of recommendation, and copies of evaluations from previous work with student teachers. In addition, these classroom teachers must meet the minimum requirements of 5 years of successful classroom teaching (as determined by the building principal), the attainment of at least a master's degree in education, the completion of at least 2 semesters of student teaching supervision in the traditional triad model, and a letter of recommendation from their principals. After this initial procedure, there is a yearly two-page reappointment application that must be submitted for the teacher to continue as a CMT. In May, the portfolios and reappointment applications are reviewed by a committee consisting of administrative personnel from the local school systems, university teacher education faculty members, and the director of clinical experiences for teacher education at UA.

## Mandatory CMT Workshop

All teachers who are newly appointed CMTs attend a mandatory 1-day summer workshop, each year, shortly before school begins. The CMT model is explained and discussed with input from many of the liaisons. During lunch, these CMTs are joined by university faculty members who teach the courses in the teacher education programs. This gives an opportunity for faculty members to circulate among the tables of CMTs and answer questions that might come up concerning content, methods, or other course work issues. It gives CMTs a chance to interact with current faculty members as well as meet new faculty who may have just been hired. After lunch the student teaching handbook is reviewed along with observation and evaluation forms. Dates and deadlines are discussed.

Later in the afternoon the workshop participants break into groups defined by teacher education programs. Faculty from each program review recent changes that affect their respective student teachers. The workshop also is a forum for the CMTs and teacher education faculty to discuss problems, concerns, or issues they might have with any aspect of the undergraduate program that would affect both groups.

The afternoon session provides an opportunity for other invited CMTs to present ways they have resolved conflicts or problems that may have arisen with student teachers during the previous year. These discussions frequently include the university liaisons, who may have played a role in helping to resolve problems or conflicts.

Since the CMTs are seeing the final products of the teacher education course work, they often have a more comprehensive view of the student teacher's readiness for all aspects of the student teaching experience. The CMT's input is a valuable contribution to the ongoing improvement of the teacher education programs.

## Student Teacher Placements

When placing student teachers in schools where a CMT team exists, we try to use all the CMT teachers at that school, if possible. Sometimes there is not a student teacher match for every member of the team; one team member may be teaching science, but there is no student teacher needing a science placement for that semester. The Office of Clinical Experiences at UA, in conjunction with several university faculty members, decides on the exact placement for each student teacher. Student teachers and their CMTs have an initial 1-hour meeting after school a day before the placement begins. This gives the CMTs a chance to acquaint the student teachers with the dress code, parking issues, check-in procedures, and directions to the individual classrooms. At this meeting the liaison is present. Times are established for the liaison to meet with the CMTs and the student teachers throughout the semester.

## Liaison Responsibilities

Every 2 weeks the liaison meets separately with the CMTs and with the student teachers. While the CMTs are meeting, the student teachers have responsibility for the students in the classroom. Meetings with the CMTs are coordinated and usually conducted by a lead teacher chosen by the CMT team. The liaison has a supportive role but does not direct the meeting. However, the liaison may deliver information from the university concerning program matters, graduation information, certification issues, or other pertinent information. After that meeting the liaison usually meets with the student teachers and is responsible for conducting the meeting. At this meeting, while issues, concerns, and problems can be addressed, the main focus is usually a discussion of the teaching opportunities and experiences the student teachers have had.

In addition to having these responsibilities, liaisons meet with the elementary or secondary school CMT coordinator once a month. The purpose of these meetings is to debrief about the progress of all the CMT teams and to ensure that all teams are adhering to the tenets of the CMT model as well as the time lines and deadlines established by the university.

## CMT Team Responsibilities

During the semester the teachers on the CMT team observe their own student teacher at least six times. They use one of the student teaching evaluation forms mandated by UA College of Education. Each evaluation form uses a point system (1–100). Six other observations are to be done by the remaining team members. The points for each evaluation are entered into the final assessment sheet and averaged together to determine the grade (A–F). However, each CMT is responsible for signing the final grade sheet on his or her assigned student teacher. The fact that the CMT holds adjunct faculty status makes the grade assignment responsibility legal under university regulations and Alabama law. When the final grades are submitted, the director of clinical experiences reviews all evaluation and assessment forms to ensure that the final grade is accurate.

If problems occur during the semester, a CMT first relies on the combined efforts of the school CMT team. If the team cannot resolve the problem, the liaison is contacted for additional input. If the problem still exists despite the help of the liaison, the CMT coordinator is brought in. So far this has happened rarely. The teams are usually able to handle problem situations satisfactorily.

An additional responsibility of the CMT team is to conduct a series of professional development seminars for the student teachers, which allows the CMTs to share areas of expertise with the student teachers; topics vary by school site. These are held once a month at the school and are led by one of the CMTs. The topics of the seminars are left up to the CMTs but have included professionalism, interviewing for a teaching position (with the CMT team acting as a site-based council), unit writing, special education services, school technology, and media services within the school or system.

## Coexistence With Traditional Model

The traditional triad model has continued to coexist with the CMT model. Usually about half the student teachers are placed with CMTs and the other half in the triad model. Not all teachers meet the requirements to be a CMT and not all cooperating teachers want to be CMTs. The traditional program is still the training ground for future CMTs. Because most of the schools used by the teacher education programs for student teachers have a CMT team, cooperating teachers in the triad model meet with the CMT team and the liaison at their biweekly meetings. However, the teachers in the triad model are not required to cross-observe the student teachers. In elementary education, the university liaison becomes the university supervisor for these cooperating teachers in the triad model at that school. In secondary education, the CMT liaison will serve as the university supervisor only for students in his or her area of content certification. The grades for student teachers in the triad model are determined jointly by the cooperating teacher and the university supervisor.

## Goals

Our first goal was to create teams of teachers within a school who would be empowered to provide support to one another as they assumed responsibility for the supervision, evaluation, and assessment of the student teachers assigned to them. As Yates (1982) indicated, student teachers believe that observations and evaluations are more valid when conducted by cooperating teachers because they are constantly in the classroom and have more intimate knowledge of the daily happenings in the classroom than the university supervisor. In addition, as Dallmer (2004) suggested, there is a need for a collegial and egalitarian relationship to be established. Typically, during the traditional student teaching experience, the role of the cooperating teacher has been passive, as they give way to their perceived expertise of the university personnel.

Our second goal was to create opportunities for collaboration between university faculty and classroom teachers that would lead to strengthening the student teaching program as well as the teacher education program. This notion was supported by the Carnegie Task Force (1986) and the Holmes Group (1990), which recommended that teachers and university faculty come together to work as a team on problems facing teacher education. To be successful, both groups must have input; they must make joint decisions on how the partnership evolves, functions, and evaluates its effectiveness; and they must have mutual trust between all stakeholders.

## HOW THE MODEL WORKS AND HOW GOALS
## WERE ACCOMPLISHED

The first goal of the CMT alternative supervision model was to develop teams of teachers at each school site. The teams would be empowered and supportive of each other as they assumed responsibility for the student teacher supervision. This goal appears to have been realized throughout the model's existence. As early as the inaugural semester of the alternative, the new CMTs demonstrated that they had "grown in self-confidence and emerged from this project with a new sense of professional importance" (Kagan & Tippins, 1993, p. 71). CMTs demonstrate a sense of ownership in the student teaching experience; the added responsibility required in the CMT model motivates them to be more engaged and empowered in the student teacher's development. As one CMT noted, "I feel more confident about the total responsibility of the grade. . . . At first I was anxious about it" (cited in Wilson & Saleh, 2000, p. 88). Although the CMTs develop confidence and empowerment, at times they feel the stress involved with the greater responsibility of serving as the adjunct faculty member who serves as the designee to assign the student teacher's final grade.

In this model, CMTs appreciate the opportunity to serve as part of a team (Daane, 2000). As one CMT noted, "As a CMT, I am able to be part of a team that works together to establish expectations of the student teachers as a whole." Elizabeth found that CMTs benefit from the support provided by other team members; this is in contrast to their relationships with the college supervisors (Wilson, 2006). One CMT explained:

> I rarely talked to the supervisor but here because I had other people in the same situation with me. . . . If I said it was a bad day, how can I say this to her to make her better. . . . It worked out a lot better. I had more support for myself. (p. 26)

This notion of support is further evidenced by the comments of another CMT: "We [the CMTs] are all here together and there is time. . . . We're just right here with each other." One student teacher exclaimed that "the CMTs were a true team!" (p. 27). The student teachers recognize that the CMTs demonstrate collegiality and a sense of community through the team supervision, the professional development seminars, and day-to-day interactions in the team and with student teacher cadres.

The empowerment and support that developed for the CMTs seems to have gone beyond supervision of the student teachers. CMTs indicate that they have become more reflective about their own teaching and supervisory practices (Kagan, Freeman, Horton, & Rountree, 1993) and perceive themselves as role models, not only for the student teachers, but also for the cooperating teachers at their schools (Wilson & Saleh, 2000).

Our second goal, creating opportunities for collaboration between university faculty and classroom teachers, was realized in ways we had not imagined. Our CMT initiative was originally established for the supervision of student teachers. However, as the model expanded to include more CMTs, we soon realized that we had more CMTs than student teachers. Since we wanted our CMTs to be involved with our students each semester, we enlisted their help with supervision with students during the semesters prior to student teaching. As enrollment in our teacher education programs grew, we realized that we needed to have more contact with local schools and more dialogue with the teachers who were supervising our students not only during student teaching, but during earlier field placements as well.

To facilitate this dialogue, the elementary education program established the Practitioner's Advisory Board, which consists of the entire 10 faculty members in elementary education and about 25 CMTs. Because of teacher schedules, not all CMTs are able to meet bimonthly, but there is usually a fairly comparable mix of university faculty and CMTs. We meet during the week from noon to 3:00 p.m., with the university paying for half-day teacher substitutes for the CMTs who attend. We are working on having representation from all the elementary schools that are involved with our teacher education program and have nearly reached that goal.

The purpose of this advisory board is to examine issues presented by either the CMTs or the faculty that relate to supervision of the students in the elementary teacher education program. One issue the CMTs presented was that the evaluation forms used by the teacher education program, prior to student teaching, were not easy to understand and use. The group as a whole worked on rewriting the evaluation forms so they were easier to understand and use and would provide better assessment of the students who were being supervised. Another bonus for the presence of CMTs on this board is that they can bring the deliberations of the board to their respective schools.

Collaborative opportunities also emerged when the enrollment in teacher education programs expanded. It became necessary to hire adjunct faculty to cover many of the courses. CMTs who were recognized by the university faculty for their pedagogical and content knowledge and supervisory expertise were invited to become instructors for the teacher education program. Some CMTs have been involved in coteaching with a university faculty member while others have been teaching with support of a faculty mentor. With either coteaching or working with a mentor, there is continuing collaboration between the CMT and the university faculty member. The CMTs have been involved in teaching the introductory courses in elementary and secondary education as well as classroom management and methods courses in language arts, reading, mathematics, and social studies. These CMT adjuncts are monetarily compensated for teaching a course. However, since all CMTs are classroom teachers, all courses must begin after the school day has ended in the local schools. The students have enjoyed learning under the direction of the CMT adjuncts because they are so close to the classroom action and can convey the realities of the classroom with much more credibility.

Collaboration also has occurred with committee work within the college of education. CMTs now sit on the Teacher Education Assessment Committee as well as the Clinical Experiences Advisory Committee. Both committees discuss issues that pertain not only to the students in the College of Education, but also to the teachers who supervise these students.

Overall, the outcomes of the CMT model have been overwhelmingly positive. As research conducted over several years shows, the goals set forth by the faculty and founders of the alternative model have been achieved. As noted by Stanford et al. (1994), this initiative has "undergone continuous revision and modification" (p. 1). Today, we continue to negotiate the dynamics of all involved in the model as we collaborate and continue to modify procedures as we have confronted challenges.

## HOW THE ALTERNATIVE MODEL CHANGED OVER TIME

As the CMT model has been implemented, it has evolved, influenced by the needs of all participants. As suggestions were made, the participants collaboratively responded and adapted policies and procedures. During the 1st years of the CMT supervision model, teams determined their level of formality or informality. As the group expanded, it was determined by the stakeholders that there was a need for greater uniformity with consistent procedures developed to do this. At that time, there were many policies and procedures that were in flux. A CMT handbook with specific procedures was thus developed and included in the annual training.

Integral to preparation for the veteran and new CMTs was the CMT summer workshop. At first, we established the 1-day summer workshop to include all CMTs, with newly appointed CMTs attending all day and veteran CMTs attending the afternoon sessions. Over time, the summer workshops became redundant for veteran CMTs, who had participated for years. With input from several CMTs, CMT liaisons, and the director of clinical experiences, it was decided that the full summer workshop would occur every 3 years instead of annually. CMTs who elect not to be reappointed for more than 1 year and then return to the model are required to attend the next summer workshop to learn about new procedures and requirements that have been implemented.

Veteran CMTs, along with the new CMTs, now participate in a fall afterschool workshop to discuss issues, concerns, and problems in the program. The director of the clinical experiences attends the workshop, to review pertinent paperwork and procedures for the upcoming school year. The fall workshop is now planned jointly with university faculty, CMTs, and liaisons, with a part conducted by CMTs, who lead a discussion on concerns and issues pertaining to all CMTs. This is a brainstorming session where everyone has an opportunity to problem-solve in a group setting.

Although the summer workshop occurs only every 3 years, it, too, has changed somewhat. An issue that emerged from research on the CMT model was assessment, particularly the final grade. In fact, when surveying 55 elementary CMTs, C. J. found that this was the most problematic aspect of being a CMT (Daane, 2000). About one third of these teachers indicated that they would have problems assigning a grade that was below a B. On a more recent open-ended survey involving CMTs, one teacher stated in response to a question on the possible drawbacks of being a CMT, "It can be hard to give negative feedback [to student teachers]." Another noted, "You are the bad guy when the student teacher is not strong." In addition to the CMTs' concerns, the university liaisons have indicated a lack of consistency with grading across teams.

To address this issue, videotapes (used with student permission) of actual teaching during methods classes or student teaching by recently graduated students are shown to both CMTs and faculty members at the summer workshop. One faculty member sits with each group of CMTs to view and evaluate the video. The evaluation forms are those used in student teaching. Each person evaluates separately, and the group then discusses the evaluation to come up with a grade consensus for the lesson. When all the groups have finished, a moderator leads them together in a discussion of the evaluation of that particular lesson. The small-group work enables faculty members to hear what classroom teachers are thinking and vice versa.

Another area of change for the CMT model is the application process. Some of the CMTs reported that when recruiting other qualified teachers in their school to apply for the alternative model, they met with resistance because of the time-consuming portfolio. In the past, potential CMTs had developed exhaustive portfolios as part of the CMT application requirements. Following feedback from CMTs and district personnel, the portfolio has been scaled back to include a few key pieces of information (such as teaching philosophy, résumé, previous student teaching evaluations, administrator recommendation, and other professional endeavors). In addition, the reapplication process has been reduced. CMTs are required to reapply each year, but the questions now focus on the applicant's accomplishments for the previous year rather than encompass the applicant's entire professional career. The forms for reapplication are now available online for the CMTs (http://education.ua.edu/clinical/cmt.html).

Few changes affecting the student teachers, have been made since most feedback from them has been positive. Given the success of the team concept and collegiality for the CMTs and the feedback from student teachers early on, the need to build collegiality in the student teacher cadres has been emphasized, especially in secondary education. There are many reasons why the secondary school student teachers need team building (e.g., student teachers may be separated by the physical layout of the school; student teachers may be involved with assisting their CMT with extracurricular activities or school duties that do not allow for interaction with others). As a result, the student teachers are encouraged to attend extracurricular activities together, dinners as a cadre with their liaison, and other social activities.

A concern that has been expressed sporadically throughout the history of the model by a few student teachers has been the notion that a CMT holds the sole responsibility for providing the final grade. This concern has been addressed and articulated clearly with the student teachers and CMTs; the final grade for the student teacher is a team decision and is based on a wide array of documentation collected throughout the student teaching experience.

## HOW THE ALTERNATIVE MODEL INFORMED OR DID NOT INFORM CHANGE TO THE TRADITIONAL MODEL

Both models of supervision are seen as equally important in our teacher education program; however, the goals of creating empowered teams and creating opportunities for collaboration are informing the triad model at our institution. On the basis of the relationships formed between CMTs and cooperating teachers, an addition has been made to enhance both models. Over time, CMTs hoped to support the cooperating teachers at their school sites and CMT coordinators wanted all student teachers at a school site to engage in similar experiences. C. J. and a colleague found that while cooperating teachers in the triad model met sporadically with other individual teachers, they still needed dialogue with all cooperating teachers on topics such as unit planning, setting expectations for student teachers, grading, and miscellaneous paperwork (Vessel & Daane, 2000). In addition, the CMTs noted three particular strengths of their meetings:

- Collaborative opportunities
- Problem-solving episodes
- Peer encouragement

At this point, the CMT model began to serve as a support for the triad model. Specifically, CMTs and cooperating teachers now meet as a team. The CMTs are able to provide guidance and support for the cooperating teachers. All student teachers, whether in the CMT or triad model, at the CMT sites are asked to attend the professional development seminars provided by the CMTs. This offers consistency as well as support for all student teachers. The engagement of the triad participants has given the cooperating teachers a training ground for the CMT model should they decide to pursue it. There are some who do not want to pursue the CMT model, since it requires greater responsibility and more documentation. In fact some CMTs have decided to return to the triad model so that they do not have the added responsibility of the paperwork and grade.

However, both groups of cooperating teachers have indicated that professional development in the area of supervision is essential to them. When C. J. and a colleague surveyed both cooperating teachers in the triad model and CMTs, they found that both groups were interested in professional development that helped them learn how to work more effectively with problem student teachers, provide constructive feedback, and conduct formal and informal observations (Vessel & Daane, 2000). As we bring the two models together for meetings in the schools, we are able to address many of these supervisory concerns. However, since only the CMTs attend the fall and summer workshops, this leaves the triad teachers out of this facet of supervisory professional development.

It is important to note that our experience has led us to recognize the importance of both models. Neither model is viewed as superior to the other. As noted by Stanford et al. (1994), "It may be that both models can flourish side by side and can contribute substantially to the professional growth of the teacher interns and school-based faculty" (p. 23). In our opinion, each model has informed the other and holds equally important status for the student teacher program at UA.

We believe that the CMT model is one that can be easily implemented if there are willing participants from both the university and the school systems where the student teachers are placed. It does take a commitment on the part of both groups to keep things running smoothly. The teachers like the autonomy, but they also like the presence of the university when the need arises. The CMT model allows the classroom teachers to feel empowered with the responsibility of supervision while receiving support from the university when needed. The collaborative nature of the CMT model allows the university faculty to interact on equal footing with the classroom teachers to create a unique supervisory model for student teaching.

# CHAPTER 5

# Using Paired Dyads with Faculty Support to Create Multiple Professional Opportunities: The Rise, Stall, and Fall of a Reform Effort

*Adrian Rodgers and Virginia L. Keil*

T HE LATE 1990s represented a critical juncture in a round of efforts aimed at reforming initial teacher preparation. (For a fuller description of the context of the 1990s, see Fullan et al., 1998.) The National Commission on Teaching for America's Future (NCTAF, 1996) documented problems and set a reform agenda; Goodlad (1994) proposed that teachers and schools were key stakeholders in renewal; and the Holmes trilogy (Holmes Group, 1986, 1990, 1995) provided a road map for how larger teacher preparation institutions could better prepare tomorrow's teachers. We had just begun new positions at The University of Toledo (UT). Adrian had just completed a doctoral degree at The Ohio State University, where he was active in an urban partnership initiative that was a part of the Holmes work, and begun his work at UT as an assistant professor. Virginia (Ginny) had recently been appointed as a member of her dean's cabinet, where she was in a position to influence the direction of UT's College of Education. She was also able to implement reforms in her new position as the director of the Office of Student Field Experiences.

Excited about the possibilities offered by our new positions, we embarked on reform-related work with excitement, tempered by the knowledge that the work would be challenging. We experienced a number of successes, including some initial innovations in supervision (Keil, Rodgers, & Switzer, 2005; Rodgers & Keil, 2007), but those innovations subsequently ended unceremoniously as UT returned to the use of a traditional supervision model. Despite the end of the implementation of our alternative model, we remained interested in redesign efforts and have been profoundly influenced by Fullan's (1993) claim that "problems are our friends" because they "are inevitable, but the good news is that you can't learn or be successful without them" (p. 25). In other words, an important part of redesign is to understand problems for the purpose of learning better ways of working, and integrating these better ways into subsequent designs. Wilson and Daviss (1994) explained that "the redesign process . . . doesn't develop without normal growing pains. . . . Such risks are expected— perhaps even necessary—during an industry's infancy" (p. 37). In our case, we encountered problems we were unable to resolve and that led to the failure of our initial effort, but we still think that we can learn from failure and that this learning can inform future work.

In this chapter we explain the disconnect between the traditional supervision model used at UT and a partnership the college of education entered into with a nearby school. Since the school was a professional development school (PDS), teachers expected close collaboration with multiple faculty members with the goal of supporting the professional development of both teachers and university faculty. In an effort to address this challenge, we will share our innovations aimed at creating a closer connection between schools and the university and discuss the effects of these innovations. Although our alternative led to deeper levels of understanding by all the participants in how to support professional growth and development, considerable university resources were required for the initial start-up phase that jeopardized the redesign effort over time. The causes of this failure will be discussed with the goal of informing future design efforts.

## A RATIONALE FOR UNDERTAKING OUR ALTERNATIVE

New faculty members at UT in the late 1990s joined a college of education well situated inside a number of reform initiatives. UT was a member of both the Great City Schools/Great City Colleges of Education collaborative and a member of the Holmes Partnership. These partnerships meant that the college had committed itself to addressing issues of urban education reform and to innovation in teacher preparation. Because of these commitments, top-level administrators, including presidents, superintendents, and deans, held the dinners, issued the press releases, and signed the memorandums of understanding committing themselves to partnership and exchanges of service. Problems arose when it came to the details regarding which services would be exchanged, and it was unclear what exactly was understood. For top-level administrators, an important and necessary mechanism for articulating partnership had been devised, but it remained for middle- and ground-level educators to decide what would further the partnership.

For us, the NCTAF (1996) report offered a succinct rallying point for articulating reform, claiming that

> new approaches connect teachers to one another through in-school teams and cross-school professional communities that tackle problems of practice over time. Though different in some respects, all of these approaches share certain features. They are
>
> • connected to teachers' work with their students
> • linked to concrete tasks of teaching
> • organized around problem solving
> • informed by research
> • sustained over time by ongoing conversations and coaching (pp. 42–43)

Given a mandate and promised modest support from top-level administrators, we saw the opportunity to devise and implement teacher education reform efforts at UT.

Fortunately, our previous professional experiences and personalities meshed well. In our teaching careers we had both successfully taught secondary English for many years in blue-collar neighborhoods. We both wanted to know more about teaching and took leaves to pursue PhDs, and perhaps because of our teaching experience, we were highly pragmatic, trusting more in what was realistic and what we thought we could accomplish and less in what administrators hoped might be accomplished. Our professional careers also meshed nicely. As the newly appointed director of the Office of Student Field Experiences, Virginia was connected to local schools, understood the shortcomings of initial teacher preparation, and knew how to get things done at the university. As a junior faculty member arriving after working on a Holmes Partnership project, Adrian had a good sense of the Holmes vision, desperately wanted to root that work in schools, and was anxious to gather and report on innovation. As individuals interested in innovation, we were grateful for the support of colleagues but also found great comfort in the support of one another in shouldering significant effort related to moving the college's commitments to reform forward. Together, we wanted to create reform initiatives that were highly connected to the work of schools and of university faculty and which were sustainable over time. Additionally we wanted to provide opportunities for professional growth for both teachers and faculty and to create a different professional vision for both teachers and faculty.

As we planned what reforms might be reasonably undertaken, we considered the other local supports that were available. There was vocal support within the college for the development of PDSs (Book, 1996) because of the history with the Holmes Partnership (Holmes Group, 1990) and because of recent and emerging scholarship on the usefulness of the PDS (Darling-Hammond, 2000; Zeichner, 1992). PDSs were first defined by the Holmes Group (1986) as schools that

> would provide superior opportunities for teachers and administrators to influence the development of their profession, and for university faculty to increase the professional relevance of their work, through (1) mutual deliberation on problems with student learning, and their possible solutions; (2) shared teaching in the university and the schools; (3) collaborative research on the problems of educational practice; and (4) cooperative supervision of prospective teachers and administrators. (p. 56)

Nevertheless, faculty were understandably extremely cautious about committing time and energy to a PDS.

Although the UT College of Education was quite large, featuring over 600 students in early childhood education (Grades PreK–3) and 200 students in middle childhood education (Grades 4–9), the adolescent and young adult (AYA) program (Grades 7–12) was smaller, with a close, collaborative faculty. Additionally, area school districts were all interested in closer collaboration with the college, especially if that collaboration could be limited in scope. Only one district wanted to commit itself to a more intense and sustained form of partnership. As these assets were reviewed, Adrian proposed a success measure called the Rule of Three. Understanding the difficulty of reform, he proposed that even if three reform efforts were undertaken and only one was implemented, success and professional satisfaction might still be claimed. With that rubric in mind, and with the support and help of multiple faculty, administrators, and area districts, the college committed itself to three sets of reforms. At the college level, we sought to develop an AYA initial teacher preparation program at the master's level (Holmes Group, 1995). At the classroom level, we sponsored initial training to establish Critical Friends Groups, a peer-to-peer support network for inquiry-oriented, reflective teachers (Achinstein & Meyer, 1997; Bambino, 2002; Franzak, 2002; Handal, 1999; Hudson, 2002; Pardini, 2000). At the college-school partnership level, we sought to develop a PDS featuring three innovations, partnering with one district willing to commit itself to substantial engagement over time.

After almost a decade of initial innovation, both the master's level teacher preparation and the Critical Friends Groups are self-sustaining, and it is only the PDS that failed, although benefits from the PDS are still being realized. Given the Rule of Three, we can still claim these reform efforts as successes! Now that we have sketched this rationale for change, we will focus on the three innovations in the PDS, with particular focus on the innovation related to an alternate model of student teacher supervision.

## A CONTEXT IN WHICH OUR ALTERNATIVE STRUCTURE WAS IMPLEMENTED

Within the 1st year of PDS work, numerous planning meetings were held with multiple stakeholders. It was proposed that the superintendent and dean meet at the beginning, middle, and end of the year to review work and that quarterly meetings between the principal and the department chair be held with the purpose of articulating supports for planning. The department chair's designee turned out to be Virginia, since she had a significant stake in the success of the work. Finally, Adrian proposed that select teachers such as department chairs or significant stakeholders and AYA faculty meet quarterly to plan work and review progress. Independently, the school district partnered with arts and science faculty, and this partnership was placed under the PDS umbrella.

It was the intent of the partnership to have buy-in from all levels of stakeholders—that senior university administrators talk to their school counterparts, midlevel administrators talk to their school counterparts, and university-level practitioners such as tenured or tenure-track faculty and clinical educators work with school practitioners such as teachers or coordinators. Upper-level partners would articulate vision and support, midlevel partners would implement and articulate support, and ground-level practitioners would undertake the work. Since ground-level practitioners worked more closely with one another and had a narrower scope of practice such as one classroom or one course, communication was as likely to be from the ground up regarding needs as it was to be from the top down regarding wants.

At the end of the 1st year, we had established a collaboration of arts and science faculty with teachers at the school, hired teachers from the school as adjunct instructors at the university, and laid the foundation of a complex, multitiered alternative to traditional student teacher supervision. The remainder of this chapter focuses on our alternative model.

### Setting

The College of Education at the University of Toledo experienced some upheaval in the late 1990s. A new dean, whose predecessor had been long serving, was appointed. Although in transition, the senior leadership of the college and university wanted to hit the ground running, and this led to fluctuations in budget that provided opportunities for those positioned to capitalize on them. Truly modest pots of money were periodically available; a willingness to try something different characterized these years, and the PDS partnership was able to take advantage of this. At the same time, as practitioners at the ground level, we were keenly aware of the shortcomings of our own supervision model, which had some of the strengths and challenges of the fictional Western Pacific University depicted in the first chapter of this book. Forms were outdated; supervision handbooks were confusing; long-serving and highly knowledgeable retired teachers served as supervisors, but they did not always understand what was being taught in methods courses on campus, which complicated feedback; most important, the primary presence the college of education had in schools was retired teachers. The college supported some stopgap measures, such as a 1-day training session for methods faculty and university supervisors in Pathwise, a trademarked observation technique developed by the Educational Testing Service. Despite this commitment to short-term professional development, we saw the opportunity to implement more complex forms of partnership. Since the college itself was restructuring, it was not a big stretch for senior administrators to support the restructuring offered by the alternative supervision model. A new principal at the prospective partner school was also setting an ambitious agenda and eager to be a part of this work.

### Participants

With 22,000 students, the University of Toledo (UT), Ohio, is a historic flagship institution with ten colleges, including those of law, business, and medicine. The college of education is a multidepartment school that enjoys a leadership role at the institution. In the case discussed in this chapter, UT partnered with the neighboring suburban Wheatfield City School District (all names of schools and school personnel are pseudonyms). Wheatfield High School (WHS) is one of two large high schools in the district, offering Grades 9–12 to a student population of 1,300 and using a teaching and support staff of about 100. Most students attending WHS are Caucasian and live in middle-, upper-middle-, and upper-income households. Although we were dedicated to supporting schools with students from blue-collar and working-class neighborhoods, we failed to obtain that level of commitment from city schools. Anxious to make headway and with significant professional commitments on the line, we opted to pursue partnership with a willing suburban district with the hope that initial success might lead to additional partnerships.

For the most part, 4 university faculty and 12 WHS staff were involved in the alternative supervision project. Science and mathematics educators, visited the school, supported the supervision alternative, and offered university course work for preservice teachers at the school. We provided additional course work and undertook the heavy lifting associated with devising and implementing our supervision alternative. The WHS teaching staff who collaborated with the university faculty were similar to their peers at the school in that they were midcareer professionals who had taught in the school district for 10–20 years. Most had master's degrees or were enrolled in master's programs, primarily at UT. We focused on English and foreign-language teachers because of the initial interest they expressed, although teachers from other areas were involved from the beginning and played increasingly important roles in the 2nd and 3rd year of the partnership.

## Data Collected

In an effort to capture two phases of the alternative supervision implementation, we gathered two sets of data. In the first phase of start-up and initial implementation, over a 4-year period we collected the following:

- Minutes of monthly meetings
- Field notes and journals recording day-to-day efforts of the collaboration
- Transcriptions of a weekly, audiotaped graduate class on supervision
- Document analyses of different documents produced by the stakeholders in the PDS, including changes to the UT supervision handbook

It was during the second phase that our alternative supervision model stalled, continuing with little to no support from the university. As our alternative model was failing, we undertook a retrospective collection of data. We collected the following:

- Retrospective narrative accounts of failure
- Time lines of key events in the stall and failure phases of the alternative
- Narratives of a new vision for university-school partnership and how this competed with the previous alternative view of supervision

Interestingly but not surprisingly, we noted there was less data to collect in this second phase partly because there was no research interest in documenting the demise of an initiative, but we take renewed interest in this now, since we have come to believe that documenting failure is highly instructive to those interested in design. This kind of investigative approach is also a way to transform something most would call failure into a redesign success story by gathering useful information for the next iteration of redesign.

## Analysis

We undertook organizing, categorizing, testing, proposing alternative explanations, and reporting data, which are the five categories of data analysis suggested by Marshall and Rossman (1995). Initially, the data source dictated the focus of the analysis. For example, when we looked at the time lines leading to stall and failure of the alternative, we also looked for other key events occurring at the school and university and how these events may have influenced the implementation of the alternative supervision model. After we categorized the data in this way, we undertook additional coding suggested by Miles and Huberman (1984). This additional coding led us to construct "analyst constructed typologies" (Patton, 1990, p. 390) which we could then test against the data. Glesne and Peshkin (1992) proposed that time spent in the field works to strengthen the trustworthiness of findings. This claim also suggests that the kind of multiyear study reported here that charts the rise, stall, and fall of an initiative can be useful for informing the work of others interested in redesign.

## THE GOALS AND STRUCTURE OF OUR ALTERNATIVE

As faculty members beginning new positions with a university that was a member of the Holmes Partnership, we were highly influenced by *Tomorrow's Teachers* (Holmes Group, 1986), which called for increased connections between universities and schools, and *Tomorrow's Schools* (Holmes Group, 1990) which proposed six principles for PDSs. We found three of these—creating a learning community; continuing learning by teachers, teacher educators, and administrators; and thoughtful, long-term inquiry into teaching and learning—to be especially helpful. We tempered idealism with careful consideration of the partner institutions and the stakeholders. Building on this thinking, we devised a number of goals. The goals for schoolchildren included opportunities to be taught by teams of teachers highly engaged in delivering quality instruction and opportunities to meet university faculty at a prospective postsecondary institution they might attend. The goals for preservice teachers included supervision by individuals highly knowledgeable about local ways of doing things, the opportunity to be known by insiders in a district who could be supportive in the hiring process and job search, and the opportunity to take course work on site without having to leave the field and return to campus. The goals for classroom/cooperating teachers included creating new roles as college instructors as well as teachers of children and the restructuring of school time to provide opportunities to work outside the classroom and with other teachers. A second set of goals for classroom teachers was to provide professional growth for veteran teachers regarding the induction of new teachers and to offer opportunities to get to know university faculty who might serve as master's advisors or faculty who might hire teachers as guest lecturers and adjunct instructors. The goals for faculty included opportunities for more connection with schools to implement research agendas related to children and student teachers. A second set of goals for faculty included opportunities to get to know teachers who might serve as master's students or who might be hired as guest lecturers and adjunct instructors and opportunities to tie the content of course work, such as methods courses, very concretely to what is being taught in schools. In addition to these goals for individuals, goals were also set for institutions. The goals for the college included greater presence in schools through partnership work, including delivery of on-site course work to preservice and inservice teachers. The goals for the schools included unique learning and professional development opportunities for children and teachers through innovative partnerships.

To accomplish these goals we devised an alternative structure we called the *paired-dyad model,* based on six key components:

1. We eliminated university supervisors who were not a part of the staff at the school.
2. We created dyads by assigning one student teacher to a cooperating teacher.
3. We took each dyad and paired it with another in the same or closely related content area and approximately the same grade level (i.e., the paired dyad).
4. We gave the role and responsibilities of the university supervisor to the cooperating teacher in the other dyad.
5. We provided graduate-level course work delivered on site to teachers who were supervising, since this was a new role for them.
6. We provided an undergraduate student teaching seminar on site to student teachers to help them negotiate the alternative supervision approach. The faculty teaching both courses also collaborated to support quality supervision.

For example, 10th-grade English teacher Ann had been assigned Arnette as a student teacher. Ann's colleague, 10th-grade teacher Brenda, had been assigned Berne as a student teacher. Using the paired-dyad model, Ann served as Arnette's cooperating teacher and Berne's university supervisor, while Brenda served as Berne's cooperating teacher and Arnette's university supervisor. Weekly, Arnette and Berne attended a student teaching seminar to discuss their work and experiences with peers and a faculty member. Also weekly, Ann and Brenda attended a graduate course in supervision to discuss their work and experiences with fellow teachers and a graduate faculty member.

## A DESCRIPTION OF HOW OUR MODEL WORKED
## AND THE GOALS ACCOMPLISHED

Although the paired-dyad model seemed very simple, it unleashed an array of opportunities and made possible the development of professional learning communities. In this section we discuss the possibilities created by our alternative model, the formation of professional learning communities around mentoring and assessment, and the importance of communication in the implementation of an alternative model.

### Possibilities Created by Our Alternative Model

Part of the usefulness of the paired-dyad model was that it built on what stakeholders already do well and provided the opportunity for flexibility so that stakeholders could undertake new work.

**Capitalizing on What Stakeholders Do Well.** In the paired-dyad model Ann and Brenda continued to serve as cooperating teachers. The student teachers continued to have the opportunity to work in depth with one cooperating teacher. University faculty continued to teach undergraduate- and graduate-level course work.

**Addressing Challenges Posed by the Traditional Model.** In this alternative—and unlike the traditional model—cooperating teachers did not have to contend with a university supervisor who may have had outdated views regarding teaching. Student teachers did not have to work with university supervisors who were disconnected from methods courses. University faculty were on site at the school, so they were more connected with school practices and had the option to drop in on student teachers to see how lessons were implemented in the classroom, and not just in theory.

University faculty also acted as consultants for special cases, but without the additional burden of accepting all the responsibilities of a university supervisor.

***Restructuring Time.*** Because Ann could leave Arnette to periodically solo teach, the former was free to act as a university supervisor to Berne, to consult with Brenda regarding issues related to classroom teaching or supervision, or to meet with other partnership stakeholders. Student teachers no longer saw returning to campus for seminars as a burden, since they were delivered on site. University faculty did not see work in schools as low-level service, since they taught courses that counted as a part of their regular load at the school.

***New Professional Opportunities.*** Ann and Brenda were hired as adjunct faculty for the university and received all the privileges of membership, including a very modest salary, parking, library access, and (importantly) a new line on their résumés. Ann and Brenda also enrolled in graduate-level course work on site that could be counted toward a master's degree or a salary increase. Since the university compensated cooperating teachers with a choice of fee waivers or cash payment, there was no additional cost incurred by the university for delivering course work on site. Faculty who wanted to be active in PDS work in a minimal way did so simply by teaching one course on site without engaging in significant other work.

***New Teaching Opportunities.*** Arnette and Berne had the opportunity to collaborate and leave the classroom in the hands of their cooperating teachers so they could team-plan lessons and return to each others' classroom to teach schoolchildren. Since university faculty were in the school building, they had the opportunity to demonstrate particular methods in class to schoolchildren, student teachers, and cooperating teachers.

***New Opportunities to Think About Teaching and Learning.*** Opportunities for debriefing include two-way debriefings between university supervisor or cooperating teacher and student teacher, or between both student teachers and both cooperating teachers. Opportunities for three-way debriefings include the cooperating teacher and university supervisor with one student teacher, or between two student teachers and one cooperating teacher. Last, there was the opportunity for a four-way debriefing between all members of the paired dyad. Cooperating teachers could work with university faculty on challenging issues over time, and student teachers could confer with university faculty in the student teaching seminar for additional explanations and conferencing.

## Formation of Professional Learning Communities
## Around Mentoring and Assessing

Although the PDS approach generally—and our alternative supervision model specifically worked well in the first 3 years of implementation—perhaps one of the most significant outcomes was the formation of a professional learning community with both faculty and teacher members. In their study of professional learning that took place in schools, Kruse, Louis, and Bryk (1995) identified five critical elements: Reflective dialogue, de-privatization of practice (or making teaching less private and more shared with peers through discussions or observation), collective focus on student learning, collaboration, and shared norms and values all contribute to effective professional learning communities (see also Supovitz, 2006; Yusko, 2004). These characteristics developed over time and with considerable emotional investment from both faculty and teachers.

*Reflective Dialogue.* During the initial 2 years of the partnership, the university offered an on-site graduate course in supervision for the cooperating teachers. As a component of this work, teachers read articles on mentoring, supervision, and partnering, and they then tried to use them to guide their work on partnership committees, which they had joined. Adrian taught these courses; he reflected with the cooperating teachers on partnering, and they reflected on the significant effort that quality partnership takes. Jane, for example, noted:

> If we're going to be cooperating [teachers], [Clinard, Ariav, Beeson, Minor, & Dwyer, 1995] suggested 3 full days of cognitive coaching seminars that teach us to do the job. [They also say] you need to have dialogue, you need to meet at least once a month with everyone that's involved with [the] process, . . . and you need to have questionnaires or journals, that you as the cooperating teacher are filling out for yourself, to improve upon your own teaching, and use this as a positive experience.

Jane's colleague Monica elaborated on this, explaining, "Every article I've read says . . . time, time, time, we don't have enough time. As teachers we need motivation for reflection, and there's nothing right now that motivates us as teachers to reflect on what we do."

One of the partnership committees decided to tackle devising criteria for selecting future cooperating teachers to be a part of paired dyads. The teachers reflected on this decision extensively, considering peers and how they were suited to work as cooperating teachers in the alternative supervision structure. At one planning meeting, one teacher suggested that teaching excellence was one essential criteria, and this initial suggestion solicited rapid-fire deliberation:

> ALTHEA: We need to put in people as mentor teachers that are looked upon, not only by their peers, but by their students, as people who are teachers . . . [who are] challenging. A mentor teacher is going to be one who obviously is reflecting on what they're doing. We want people [as mentors] who are constantly progressing with education—to new techniques and teaching.
>
> BERNICE: [I'm] not saying that one teacher's better than another, but [we need to say] this is what we want you to do. For example, [we need to ask prospective cooperating teachers], "Do you want to learn not only how to perfect your own ability to develop a lesson, but how to coach somebody to do the same thing? . . . Are you interested in guiding a person through the process?"
>
> CANDACE: In some of the articles [I've read], collaboration was important: Are you willing to work with other teachers? Do you want to discuss the teaching process? Do you want to reflect on the process itself?
>
> ALTHEA: Are you willing to preconference? Are you willing to postconference? Are you willing to attend group meetings with your cooperating teachers so you can all work the problems through?
>
> CANDACE: Are you willing to reflect on your own teaching?
>
> ALTHEA: We need to set what we want to see as the standards at our school. Schoon and Sandoval (1997) [said that in partnerships] schools have the ability to say to the university that we want these things from the candidates who will be coming to us: Lots of time in reflecting, more supervision in earlier field experiences before getting to a professional development school, and more of a connection with methods faculty and the school.

In addition to selection criteria for prospective cooperating teachers, this same committee also revised the university's student teaching handbook and forms used for evaluating student teachers. Virginia supported the teachers, suggesting components that she had found helpful in her own supervision work in the past. Based on this, the teachers decided they would document four observations with written narratives, complete a formal midterm and final conference, and select five other options from the list in Figure 5.1. In terms of Option 2 in Figure 5.1, when they use scripting, cooperating teachers meant they would either record in writing everything the student teacher and children said during a lesson, or they would target their observation around a particular feature—such as the questions posed during a lesson—and script those responses. A dialogue or trialogue journal was a reflective journal divided in two or three columns where the student teacher, cooperating teacher, and sometimes the university supervisor might write. Similarly, Options 3, 4, and 5 analyzed specific ways the student teacher interacts with the children being taught. As a part of these reflections, Adrian learned that not all cooperating teachers and university supervisors agreed on performances of student teachers. He suggested that observation forms include a check box indicating that there were differing viewpoints; checking this box would trigger an additional observation by a third party such as a university faculty member.

Although a lot of reflective dialogue occurred between teachers, the new role of university supervisor that they were adopting meant that they also had to confer with university faculty to better understand expectations. This was especially the case with grading, which was a very new task for the teachers. At one meeting, Virginia explained:

> The perception is one that all student teachers have been given A's. Not true. They have been earned, not given. Percentage-wise, we are probably looking at 60% getting A's. Every semester we loose a total of 10–12 student teachers [out of 400], and then the rest fall in the realm of a B or C.

This caused one teacher to ask about grade inflation at the university, saying she'd heard some student teachers say that the B they received for

**Figure 5.1.** Options for supervision.

---

1. Four narratives

2. Engagement observation, with a choice of scripting or dialogue journal

3. Behavior intervention analysis

4. Analysis of nonverbal communication

5. Interaction analysis

6. Formal midterm evaluation

7. Formal final evaluation

---

student teaching was the only B they had ever got. This caused Adrian to note that grade inflation was not unique to the college of education and that 80% of a student's courses and therefore the student's grades were issued by arts and sciences faculty rather than education faculty. Virginia added, "If you put A's on everybody, you're sending the message that everyone is the same, and they're not." One teacher concluded, "This is the whole purpose of the PDS because we want to raise the profession and raise the quality. This is tough for us—we've never done this before, but I think we'll be better next year."

***Deprivatization of Practice.*** Kruse et al. (1995) suggested that a second critical element underpinning effective professional learning communities is the deprivatization of practice. A critical issue in the start-up phase of the alternative supervision model was communication between all the stakeholders. At the end of the 1st year, one teacher reflected,

> We have improved, ongoing communication and this process is positive and is very constructive. There is a lot of feedback; the evaluations [of student teachers] are better and ongoing; some of the conflicts between supervising and cooperating teachers have been reduced. Supervisors are [at three-way conferences] to explain what they mean in their written evaluations which is beneficial. [There are also communication benefits to being in ongoing contact. For example,] I've raised some concerns with a student teacher [I supervise], and he said to come back [later in the day], and he would give the lesson another shot with another class he taught. So I came in later that same day, and [because I was already at the school] I had the freedom to do that and was able to see him implement and improve on some of the things I had commented on.

***Collective Focus on Student Learning.*** Although Kruse et al. (1995) were thinking of child learning when they wrote about this component, in the alternative supervision model the focus on learning was on student teacher learning. After the 1st year of the initiative, both teachers and university faculty suggested an approach to more customized placement of student teachers. Virginia suggested interviews prior to placement in which cooperating teachers could ask questions gauged to customize the match between student teachers, cooperating teachers, and university supervisors. Some of the sample questions she recommended are listed in Figure 5.2.

In addition to customizing the match, teachers wanted to expand the penetration of the university at the school. For example, one teacher reflected,

**Figure 5.2.** Sample interview questions focusing on customizing teacher/student teacher match.

---

• With what kind of mentor would you like to work?

• What is your basic presentation/teaching style?

• Do you need a lot of praise?

• Do you need a lot of structure?

• Are you a self-starter?

• Do you take criticism well?

---

> I would like to see Adrian and his methods students take a more active role at the school: observing classes, planning and participating in activities, working with teachers at the school. I am pleased with the PDS progress. I think our next big project should be to coordinate UT methods classes with school teaching instruction on site.

***Collaboration.*** Although some cooperating teachers wanted to expand the scope of the partnership with the goal of expanding student learning, other teachers were keenly aware of the delicate nature of partnership work. It was interesting to see how things changed from the razzle-dazzle of the very first partnership meeting featuring senior administrators and media to the end of the 1st year of substantive partnership. One teacher who had been there throughout the 1st year wrote in her reflective journal:

> My first few months teaching at the school were exciting, even more so after I found out the university was interested in a partnership.
>
> The school was very excited and the university was very professional. Imagine: They wanted to work with us, and we are just teachers. What could we possibly offer them? We sat down for dinner at the Hyatt and just talked. We talked about what the ideal classroom was and how we could work to get it. The dean got up and made a speech and told us how we were laying the foundation for education and that we were going to be the model for schools in the area. We were promised $20,000 from the university, and the university was promised our full collaboration. . . .

We had our next meeting. It was well attended by the university, but the school did not show. One of the school's committee members also did not show. This was embarrassing and humiliating. Adrian was optimistic about it, but I was frustrated. How could my colleagues do this? What happened to the 15 people who had wanted to sit on the committee? It was obvious that Virginia was very disappointed in the school turnout as well. . . .

The partnership went through cycles. . . . The questioning phase continued throughout the year; teachers were always asking me what was in it for them. The most distressing phase, failure, was where I thought we should just give up. The student teachers weren't happy, UT was hearing many complaints, and the cooperating teachers weren't getting the support they felt they deserved from UT. I had to stumble and push forward. . . . I decided to put myself in the role of communications coordinator. . . . Things did start to look up. The final meeting between UT and the school was not well attended, but it was attended by the key players—the people who believe in the partnership and want to see it continue.

***Shared Norms and Values.*** Interestingly, each cooperating teacher and each faculty member had many years of teaching experience, so they all shared a common set of professional norms regarding professional expectations. Although they shared this common set of values, cooperating teachers found the new roles they were adopting as university supervisors uncomfortable and unusual. For example, one student teacher was chronically late in arriving at the field. In a traditional supervision setting, a university supervisor would have intervened after the second late arrival, but the teachers who served in their new role of university supervisor felt uncomfortable with these heavy-handed tactics, so they delayed action. Eventually, Candace found herself writing the letter in Figure 5.3. When Virginia learned that such a letter was even necessary and that Candace had waited so long, Mr. Smithely was called in for a four-person meeting and was informed that he was at risk to not pass student teaching; any additional late arrivals at the school would result in immediate removal from the field experience.

Although all could agree on how to handle a poorly performing beginning teacher, negotiating differences between colleagues who were acting as cooperating teachers and university supervisors was much more delicate. Virginia explained:

When the student teacher leaves the school we have two colleagues that are still there, still teaching side by side, that have to

**Figure 5.3.** Candace's letter to a late-arriving student teacher.

---

Dear Mr. Smithely,

It is with great concern that I write this letter of formal reprimand. The irresponsible and unprofessional behavior exhibited and documented on January 21, January 26, February 5, and March 1 are unacceptable for any teacher. Reporting to the job late or without advance notification leaves the students unsupervised, which in turn creates a liability risk for you as well as the school you represent. . . .

---

find a way to continue the school year. And we can't forget: If a rift has developed in this process because of a breakdown in communication between colleagues, we'll need to put communication mechanisms in place so that people are not put in corners.

One faculty member suggested that student teachers needed an advocate and that the advisor could intervene with students who were not meeting professional challenges. Reflecting on her intervention with one student who was struggling with student teaching, she explained:

> As an advisor I'm the one who brought the tears flowing that day. I did the confrontation. I said, "A problem's been brought to my attention, and we need to talk." We want to be solicitous in having the faculty advisor work with the student.

Although the groundwork had been set for a robust and rich professional learning community, little did stakeholders know that multiple factors would soon destroy it.

## CHANGES OVER TIME

The 3rd year of the partnership met many challenges. At the university level, Adrian moved to a new faculty position at a different university, and Virginia was promoted from the director of the Office of Student Field Experiences to associate dean of the college. A new student teaching director who was well known and liked at the university, but who had little experience in student teaching supervision, was appointed. At the same time, the previous college dean was replaced by a new dean who faced NCATE accreditation for the college as his first challenge. During that 3rd year there would also be significant changes at the school, including a rotation of assistant principals and principals before a permanent administration was put in place.

These changes posed significant challenges for the student teaching office. It was a big stretch for them to work extensively with one school, support cooperating teachers in continuing their past practices with highly customized placements, and identify how faculty could support teachers and train them to supervise student teachers.

As other faculty were called in to fill the void left by Adrian and Virginia, there was recognition of the considerable amount of work involved. Since this work was less connected with the research agendas of other faculty and because the senior faculty had different content expertise from that of most of the teachers involved in the partnership who were at the school, interest by university faculty declined. While it was difficult for other faculty to maintain contact with the teachers at the school, it was also difficult for Virginia to maintain her involvement. She explained:

> Although I had an interest in maintaining the Professional Development School, it was difficult to maintain oversight of the student teaching office and fulfill all of my new professional responsibilities. With all of the school and university transitions, there was little or no understanding on the part of the student teaching office regarding the relationships that had been built. So the teachers felt somewhat alienated or disenfranchised because the field office was trying to simply move back into the old model.

Although there may have been interest by teachers in maintaining the alternative supervision model, the leadership of the school had become interested in Schools That Work (www.schoolsthatwork.org; see also Wood, 1992). Virginia summarized this as a renewal initiative based on teachers and administrators taking a hard look at data in order to improve student learning. This initiative competed with our alternative supervision model because our alternative model placed a number of student teachers at the school, which could be perceived as interfering with teaching children. Virginia explained:

> I think there was a perception on the part of the teachers that if they were working with a student teacher, they needed to do it much more closely and do much more guiding in the process. You could look at this as very positive because they were truly trying to be mentors, but then they were conflicted when they needed to act as summative evaluators.

Even the offering of the on-site undergraduate student teaching seminar was eventually terminated because the university didn't have enough student teachers in the building or in that area of town to make it worthwhile.

Finally, the newly arrived permanent principal decided that teachers were playing multiple roles as supervisor and cooperating teacher and that it was problematic because of scheduling. At that point, after 6 years, our alternative supervision model was abandoned by the principal.

It may seem strange that one person could finalize the dénoument of a multiyear partnership, but Wilson and Daviss (1994) suggest that it is quite typical of education innovation. They explain:

> [In industry, the] redesign process . . . doesn't develop without normal grow-ing pains. . . . Such risks are expected—perhaps even necessary—during an industry's infancy. A redesign process grows and strengthens by allowing people to work through those failures while an industry is still young. From one model change to the next, redesign allows engineers to identify failure's causes and "design out" the flaws that lead to disaster. . . . But not in the schools. . . . The reason isn't hard to determine: education has no redesign process that allows it to build on its past experience of change. Every expe-rience in implementing an innovation is new, alien, approached as if it had never been done before. No broad vision infuses each task of educational change with a sense of context and continuity; no organizational culture or systematized process of change supports or guides educators as they cast about for better ways to do things. Education still confuses changing a program or procedure with the process of change itself. (pp. 37–38)

They add, "Career mobility also works against the program. Whether in a corporation or a school district, any innovation needs a high-level champion. . . . Without a champion, the innovation can get lost in a gaggle of competing initiatives" (p. 73).

## HOW OUR ALTERNATIVE MODEL
## INFORMS THE TRADITIONAL MODEL

Although our alternative supervision model eventually failed, the devel-opment of this Professional Development School and our alternative su-pervision model still helped the university increase the sophistication of its supervision. One valuable change was the development of a series of documents to assist students and cooperating teachers in understanding university programs and student expectations. One new document, "Be-coming a Teacher at the University of Toledo" starts with the 1st year of study and explains how the university will assess undergraduate students as well as the developmental stages of becoming a teacher all the way through to the development of a student teaching portfolio. Each student now has a handbook explaining these steps.

Additionally, there is a higher expectation in the criteria that supervisors must meet, including a screening process featuring multiple interviews where supervisors consider expectations and student teacher assessment requirements. Although our alternative model was piloted with only upper-grade teachers, when the lessons of our alternative model were applied to the traditional model, the university was able to generalize the lessons learned to the preparation of teachers for all grades.

There were other lessons learned by the university and its faculty. As Virginia explained, faculty were made

> painfully aware of the amount of work it takes to establish partnerships initially. It is not simply a matter of go in and get started. You are going to spend several years just getting to know each other and learning how to trust each other.

A second factor included the cultural differences between institutions. As Virginia remarked in an interview:

> We are from different cultures and that's a huge issue. If anything, I think our partners, those teachers who were intimately working with us for a period of time, truly began to understand that cultural difference. Faculty, who had served as teachers, understood the routines and pressures of the teaching world. I don't think teachers, because they had not lived in the world of a faculty member, truly have a grasp of what it means to move through tenure and promotion. I still run into Candace, and she still talks about when Adrian went and taught her students, and I think I would move those pieces to the forefront. They are clearly critical pieces that we didn't spend enough time looking at.

From her reflections, Virginia has identified several possibilities for future partnerships. First, the possibility of faculty actually teaching in high school classrooms so that multiple things could happen is useful. Both content specialists and pedagogical experts could participate, thus providing teachers with professional development opportunities and students with exposure to college professors. A second component is the re-visioning of promotion and tenure requirements to include school partnership work. As Virginia explains, "I see faculty who are very, very focused on tenure and promotion, and the fact remains that this sort of work is still not deemed as credible for promotion unless the work is published. Until there are some huge shifts in the paradigm, it will forever be a problem because for most senior faculty, a professional development school is just not part of the mix." In addition to these two cultural possibilities, there are four structural possibilities. First, the assignment of district superintendents to university advisory panels would help. Second, the identification of funds for the establishment of magnet schools with significant university involvement would be of assistance. Third, the recruitment of cooperating teachers who are involved in alternative supervision models to come and teach undergraduate classess at the university would be useful. Finally, the development, from the outset, of an exit plan that would guide the dissolution of a partnership between university and school partners would be essential. This would reduce stakes and support the maintenance of mutual respect through the inception, life, and death of partnership work.

## LEARNING FROM PARTNERSHIPS

Partnerships are complex, unique collaborations with multiple stakeholders, varying needs, and differing degrees of sophistication. Readers learned in Chapters 3, 4, and 5 of this book that some partnerships may last and reap benefits for all stakeholders. However, readers have also learned that even so-called failed partnerships can be highly instructive for reform efforts. In Chapters 6 and 7, we look across the three cases discussed in this book, consider similarities and differences between cases, and consider how these cases can be useful for considering future partnership work.

# The Implications of Using
# Alternative Models

# CHAPTER 6

# Using Structure and Culture as Tools for Examining Success and Failure: A Cross-Case Analysis

*Adrian Rodgers*

THE TEACHING COMMISSION (2006) recently released its report *Teaching at Risk: Progress and Potholes*, which identified four domains for reform including reinventing teacher preparation. Although this document is in a long line of reports that call for reform, reform remains difficult to accomplish. Why is this the case and what can be done to change the likelihood of success in change initiatives? In this chapter I adopt the structural and cultural interpretive lens advocated by Fullan (2007); look across the three cases discussed in Chapters 3, 4, and 5; and examine why faculty at each institution either succeeded or failed in their reform efforts. The structural and cultural components that were in place at Brigham Young University (BYU) and The University of Alabama (UA) supported the alternative model. At The University of Toledo (UT), faculty put in place structural components to support success, but they could not fully anticipate some of the cultural customs that would eventually undermine the use of the fledgling alternative model.

## USING STRUCTURE AND CULTURE AS A TOOL FOR ANALYSIS

With the insight offered by decades of reform efforts, Fullan (2007) can now write that "changing working conditions, in common with all successful organizational change, involves two components, structure and culture" (p. 292). In this section the characteristics of structure and culture are described, and the complexity of shaping these characteristics to accomplish change is considered. It should be pointed out that these characteristics are not the only characteristics relevant to structure and culture, but they are useful in looking across cases, so users should not consider them as a checklist, but rather as an introductory tool to support thinking regarding partnerships interested in change.

Fullan (2007) used two major sets of conditions for Professional Learning Communities identified by Kruse et al. (1995) as a way of discussing reform efforts. "One is 'structural'—in particular, time to meet and talk, physical proximity, interdependent teaching roles, communication structures, and teacher empowerment and school autonomy" (p. 149). In other words, structural conditions include use of time (such as time in the day to collaborate and time in the semester for planning); arrangement of stakeholders in buildings (for example, within the school) and between buildings (for example, distance between a school and the university); overlapping work (for example, cooperating teachers working as university supervisors); and ways of working together and talking to one another on a case-by-case basis, and ways to communicate from one person or working group to the whole group.

In summary, using this helpful list would suggest that school-university partnerships active in devising alternative supervision models would want to create opportunities for common planning, consider the importance of proximity between the within-school partners and between the school and university, look for opportunities for stakeholders to optimize work duties to capitalize on the restructuring, develop communication avenues, and consider the power relationships that allow for a range of work from fully independent to fully collaborative.

Fullan (2007) goes on to say that

> the other condition is what Kruse, Louis, and Bryk call "social and human resources" (or what we refer to as culture) and includes openness to improvement, trust and respect, cognitive and skill base, supportive leadership, and socialization (of current and incoming staff). They claim, as I do, that the structural conditions are easier to address than the cultural ones. (p. 149)

In other words, cultural conditions also include interest in and willingness to explore change that might lead to improvement; faith in one another's judgment; knowledge about change, supervision, and quality teaching, and the ability to put this knowledge into action; leaders interested in promoting and aiding the alternative supervision approach; and opportunities for current and incoming staff to buy into the reforms by learning about them and trying them out.

This list of points considering cultural characteristics would suggest that school-university partnerships active in alternative supervision would want to consider identifying interested faculty and school personnel, ensuring that the stakeholders involved are highly regarded both within the organization and by others outside the organization, activating opportunities to develop knowledge and skills, identifying and recruiting leaders into the initiative and sustaining this leadership over time, and creating renewal opportunities for current and incoming staffers.

But Fullan (2007) adds one important caveat to this characterization of structure and culture that users will want to consider. When considering structure and culture, Fullan elaborates on the relationship between the two:

> The former [structure] is important but also the easier of the two. Thus, providing more time for teachers to work together during the day, as many jurisdictions are doing, is necessary but not sufficient. If the capacity (culture) is not evident in these situations, the new time will be squandered more times than not. . . . In sum, new policies that promulgate high standards of practice for all teachers invite the possibility of large-scale reform. A corresponding set of policies is required to create many opportunities, in fact requirements, for people to examine together their day-to-day practice. It is through local problem solving with expanded horizons that new solutions can be identified and implemented. This represents a huge cultural change for schools, and as such it is going to require sophisticated new leadership. (pp. 292–293)

In other words, features such as time, physical arrangements, and the way in which the work of stakeholders overlaps is important and will need to be considered. In addition to this, effort will need to be invested in building willingness to change, providing opportunities for buy-in, building faith in one another's knowledge and skill, and recruiting leaders who are invested in reform.

## THE STRUCTURE OF ALTERNATIVE
## APPROACHES TO SUPERVISION

Using the work of Fullan (2007) and Kruse et al. (1995), I looked across all three cases at the structural features each partnership had in common. These are depicted in Table 6.1. When observers look across the three cases, the BYU model relies on quality placements which can support two student teachers, while the UA model relies on specially trained supervisors who fulfill multiple roles. The UT model was more complex. It relied on multiple course offerings being delivered on site at one school and an arrangement of two cooperating teachers and two student teachers working together in a very different way. The cooperating teachers and university faculty had different roles, and the UT model relied upon a lot of

**Table 6.1.** Structural characteristics across cases.

| Structural Conditions | Brigham Young University (Chapter 3) | The University of Alabama (Chapter 4) | The University of Toledo (Chapter 5) |
|---|---|---|---|
| Use of time | STs can collaborate<br><br>One CT can work with two STs simultaneously | Training period at beginning of year sets expectations<br><br>Liaison can meet with CMTs while STs teach | Paired dyads support multiple conferencing opportunities<br><br>District and university support PD Days |
| Arrangement of stakeholders | Multiple sites; exists alongside traditional supervision<br><br>Fewer high-quality placements need to be found<br><br>Two STs in one classroom | Multiple sites; exists alongside traditional supervision<br><br>Changes in US role emphasize importance of CT<br><br>Usually many CMTs at each site<br><br>Continuing faculty input | One site; exists alongside traditional supervision<br><br>Systems approach to partnership<br><br>CT can take on multiple roles because of partnership with adjoining CT |
| Overlapping work | STs work extensively in small groups<br><br>Some STs desire more time to teach | PD Seminars led by CMTs<br><br>Collegial support among CMTs = peer collaboration | CT has multiple roles<br><br>Delivery of on-site course work for CTs and STs |
| Ways of working and talking together | STs can talk and plan together<br><br>Exponential growth in ideas | Practitioner Advisory Board<br><br>Interrater reliability established through viewing of videotapes<br><br>ST grade as a team decision | Existing structure (ST Seminar) supports debriefing of alternative structure<br><br>Deletion of university-based US flattens communication |
| Degree to which stakeholders can work independently and together | Opportunities to work more independently or more collaboratively across different classrooms<br><br>Collegiality | Use of the traditional model as a training ground for the CMT model<br><br>CMTs are instructors in the teacher education program | Each paired dyad can customize relationship<br><br>CTs, STs, faculty, and school personnel can test innovations at the local level |

support from the district to supply release time for professional development days. While this was reliably supported in the beginning years, this was difficult to sustain in succeeding years.

In all cases, the alternative model never replaced the traditional model but instead was instituted alongside it. Both BYU and UA were quickly able to use their model in multiple sites, but the complexity of the UT model restricted its implementation to one site. In retrospect, this may have placed a lot of control on the way the alternative model happened to work in one particular site, but it limited replication in other schools and districts. This would subsequently mean that the future of the UT alternative model would ride on one school.

A key to all three alternative supervision models was the careful articulation of stakeholders so that they could work in proximity to one another and build on the creativity of each team. Since the three models relied on ongoing collaboration, faculty at all three institutions paid a lot of attention to how the work of the stakeholders could overlap. For example, BYU relied on partnership between student teachers and the cooperating teacher; UA relied on collaboration in a fall conference, with continuing faculty input throughout the year; and UT relied on collaboration among faculty, teachers, and student teachers. In all these collaborations, cooperating teachers had significant and increased roles. To support these new roles, some models had to devise new ways of talking with one another while other sites built on existing communication tools.

Despite this emphasis on new roles for the cooperating teacher, all the models relied on cooperating teachers working closely together with the goal of customizing the way in which cooperating teachers could work with the student teachers they supervised. A key component of these structures is careful collaboration among stakeholders. The BYU model relies on careful collaboration within the classroom between two student teachers and a classroom teacher; the UA model relies on the clinical master teacher working carefully with peers, including other teachers and faculty; and the UT model relies on cooperating teachers, student teachers, and faculty working carefully with one another. These socialization processes are significant. For example, in Goodlad's (1990) comprehensive investigation of 29 universities, one of his main findings was that preparation programs made little use of the socialization process used in other professional preparation. As Fullan (2007) concluded, "This relatively isolated individualism in preparation seems ill-suited to developing the collegiality that will be demanded later in site-based school renewal" (p. 269). Alternative student teaching supervision models rely carefully on site-based collegiality.

The collegiality on which alternative sites rely supports interrater reliability between observers, or more specifically, observers arriving at similar conclusions based on the same observations. For example, in the UA model a team is responsible for the grade of student teachers. Meanwhile, at UT, two cooperating teachers in the university supervisor role collaborate with the option to call in faculty assistance. The significance of cooperating teachers and faculty arriving at similar conclusions is important. Student teachers need to be assured that the grades and comments they receive are reflective of expert opinions rather than the whim of one individual or the luck of the draw. This issue becomes increasingly important if universities attempt to scale up their work across multiple school sites; as readers have already learned, quality classroom placements can be hard to find (Walkington, 2007). For these reasons, the application of the same standards and the same quality of feedback across sites and personnel is important, since standardization supports sustaining a network of alternative sites.

Of course, there are challenges associated with changing traditional relationships. For example, high-quality cooperating teachers do not always want to adopt additional roles related to supervision. They may be eager to host a student teacher but not especially interested in the summative comments and additional responsibilities of the university supervisor. For this reason, care must be taken to not lose great cooperating teachers when implementing an alternative supervision model. This is important, since the principal role of student teachers is to teach their students, so the additional responsibilities that come with alternative supervision roles must always be considered with caution. Challenges are also posed for university professors, because the elimination of supervision responsibilities may inadvertently lead to the obsolescence of teacher educators. For these reasons, alternatives must be designed and tested rather than adopted without careful and cautious consideration.

## THE CULTURE OF ALTERNATIVE
## APPROACHES TO SUPERVISION

As with structural features, it is also possible to use the work of Fullan (2007) and Kruse et al. (1995) to look across all three cases at the cultural features the partnerships have in common. These are depicted in Table 6.2. Of the three cases, the BYU model relies on the promise offered by working with two student teachers, who, of course, represent twice as much intellectual power and double the collaborative power with students. UA, meanwhile, has multiple school personnel interested in supporting student teachers as mentors to the profession. The UT model, however, relies on sustained interest by school faculty, who, of course, had multiple professional roles to fulfill. A feature of all three alternative models is that they rely on unique articulations of trust, with the UT model relying on trust within each of the paired dyads and between these paired dyads and university faculty. UA, meanwhile, restricts its collaborations to carefully selected licensed teachers and interested faculty, while BYU focuses its partnerships on collegiality at the classroom level.

**Table 6.2.** Cultural conditions across cases.

| Cultural Conditions | Brigham Young University(Chapter 3) | The University of Alabama (Chapter 4) | The University of Toledo (Chapter 5) |
|---|---|---|---|
| Interest/willingness to explore change | Added CT role of supervising 2 STs offset by benefits of additional ST present<br><br>Open to innovation beyond ST experience | Prospective CMTs apply for CMT role<br><br>New professional roles for CMTs | Initial high level of interest at all levels of university and school<br><br>Eroding interest of higher-level administrators in complex change; competing interests for ground-level faculty |
| Faith in one another 's judgment | Enhanced trust by CTs of STs<br><br>Social and emotional support<br><br>Tension yields to collaboration | Selection criteria for CMTs<br><br>Emphasis on CMT team to address problems<br><br>CMTs work carefully with peers | CTs work closely with one another<br><br>CTs consult faculty when facing problems<br><br>STs have the opportunity to conference with one another |
| Knowledge and skill | Enhanced classroom management<br><br>Enhanced student learning | CMTs teach introductory courses<br><br>CMTs sit on Teacher Education Assessment Committee | Challenges in the development of new knowledge and skills for CTs<br><br>High level of emphasis on situated learning |
| Leadership | Changes and shifts in power relationships between CT and STs<br><br>Issues localized to classroom leadership issues | Administrators included in selection of CMTs<br><br>Leadership of the program at the university level | Buy-in initially obtained from top-, middle-, and ground-level school and university faculty but . . .<br><br>. . . no mechanism for renewal when key personnel leave or transfer |
| Buy-in for current and incoming staff | Supervising two STs is transformative for the CT<br><br>STs may feel that paired teaching is not realistic | One day of training per year<br><br>CMTs share solutions to technical problems annually<br><br>Alternative faculty role | Initial course offerings support buy-in, but...<br><br>. . . no mechanism for newly arriving teaching staff |

The support of knowledge and skill development varies across sites. For example, the BYU alternative does not feature any kind of significant training, but the UA model features a selection process and a 1- to 3-day preparation process. In some ways UT has the most complicated selection process, relying on the completion of a graduate course in supervision, but the UT model does not have a self-sustaining model for subsequent years of testing the alternative. In other words, once teachers have completed the graduate course, there is no organized way for them to meet as a whole group in subsequent years. Perhaps because of this, there is also no structured way to support an ongoing reculturation process, something that UT eventually struggled with.

The leadership models of the BYU and UA models are also simpler but more effective in that they rely on classroom level or university level interventions. The buy-in of leadership in the UT model is much more complex, but that makes it prone to failure if the leaders change. The UT model relies on significant supports from the building-level principal and from senior-level college administrators. When both the principal and the college administrators changed, there was no mechanism to cultivate support from the new leadership. Further, a lot of the onus for leadership at the middle and ground levels of the partnership fell on two faculty, Adrian and Virginia. When Adrian accepted a new position at a different university and Virginia was promoted, critical ground-level leadership was lost. Thus, the faculty had not succeeded in reculturing the partnership to the point that other faculty could easily step in and take up the leadership piece. This issue was exacerbated by the problem of there being no ongoing mechanism for the buy-in of current and incoming teaching staff. Since the new faculty leadership had no mechanism to collaborate with teachers, it was easy to abandon the partnership. This is in sharp contrast to the BYU and UA models, which have mechanisms for ongoing support.

Although UT did have limitations in the support of cultural features that would have supported the implementation of the alternative model, what is significant about the trends across the alternative sites is the movement to increased empowerment of cooperating teachers and the development of more robust partnerships between schools and universities. This empowerment comes at some cost. For example, not all cooperating teachers are comfortable adopting the role of both evaluating student teachers and providing emotional and technical support. Similarly, in these new alternative supervision models, university faculty are less likely to fulfill traditional roles as supervisors related to content and pedagogy and they are more likely to be experts in cultural change as they oversee and facilitate the change process and lay the groundwork for and monitor change. This shift requires a different way of viewing professional development. In a partnership model, professional development evolves over time and is carefully tailored to partner needs. This is different from teaching in a time-limited course in which the agenda is set by the faculty member, a curriculum committee, or NCATE requirements. Engaging in partnerships is different from another task faculty often perform—presenting a session at a teacher conference. Presenting a one-shot workshop at a teaching conference comes with the assumption that the faculty member has expert content knowledge, that this knowledge is sought by the attendees, that the faculty is to communicate this knowledge to the attendees, and that the conference session is time limited. In other words, when faculty present at a teacher conference it really is "stand and deliver." This is very different from partnership work. Faculty involved in partnerships need a knowledge base in organizational behavior to complement their content knowledge and require an additional skill set in working in partnerships over time. In partnerships, expert knowledge is held by all stakeholders and needs to be weighed and deliberated, so group consensus can set the agenda and make decisions. Thus, faculty adept at teaching may not necessarily fare well in partnerships if they are not willing to rethink the power relationships that are a part of this very different culture.

As university faculty shift into new roles, some institutions will be more flexible at handling change than others. Smaller and medium-sized institutions, with fewer stakeholders, may be more adept at handling changes in structure and culture than larger institutions, where multiple stakeholders may inadvertently challenge redesign processes. In the simplest terms, too many cooks may not spoil the broth, but they may spend so much time deliberating over the contents that nothing gets done. Another factor that may influence structural and cultural shifts are the values on which teacher preparation programs are based. For example, the degree to which teachers and faculty agree on the importance of conceptual underpinnings, such as constructivism, cultural relativism, pedagogical content knowledge, developmental theories, and skills and apprenticeship, will influence alternative supervision models. In summary, regardless of how much attention is paid to the structure of an alternative supervision approach, the alternative very well may fail, without a careful consideration of the cultural factors at work. This is all the more problematic because cultural factors are hard to define and understand and are in some ways out of the control of those interested in redesign. Put another way, you can set a time for a meeting, but if the participants do not want to be there you will have a problem.

Perhaps one of the reasons that these reculturing efforts are so difficult is that teacher preparation institutions themselves reinforce traditional cultural assumptions rather than rewarding reculturing. Professional and institutional recognition continues to be offered for the sole authored, experimental, peer-reviewed study that is limited in size and duration rather than the messier, collaborative, descriptive work that captures and characterizes partnership. Despite this reinforcement of the traditional

reward structure, reward structures within teacher preparation departments continue to be problematic when compared with the rest of the
university. Fullan (2007) explained:

> The Teaching Commission (2006) gave a grade of *D* in its section on "Rein-
> venting Teacher Preparation." The commission concludes that there are few
> incentives to improve initial teacher education. There is little political in-
> centive to tackle the problem seriously. Universities by and large have failed
> to mobilize their institutional resources to revamp teacher education. (p. 275)

Clearly, with increased scrutiny and accountability measures, teacher
education institutions will either need to confront change or run the risk
of being put out of business.

## ACHIEVING GREATER SUCCESS WITH
## ALTERNATIVE SUPERVISION APPROACHES

What is significant about all three alternative supervision approaches is
that they all place an emphasis on initial and ongoing professional learning. When Morris and Hiebert (2009) examined other professions and their
attempts to improve practices, they looked at the "interactions and learning of the people in the professions rather than [at] the products they produce or services they provide" (p. 430). This is important because educators
often look at products (student test scores) or services (staffing and competencies) rather than initial and ongoing professional learning.

Morris and Hiebert (2009) began by identifying four features of knowl-
edge-building systems that appear critical for making progress outside of
education:

1. shared goals across the system
2. visible, tangible, changeable products
3. small tests of small changes
4. multiple sources of innovation from throughout the system (pp. 431)

In the following sections I apply these four features to teacher education,
discussing the relationship among them and between the success or failure experienced at each of the three sites.

### Success

Let's begin by considering how all three supervision models were able to
build on the four features articulated by Morris and Hiebert (2009) to

achieve success. The first feature was a shared goal, where collaboration was seen as an advantage. Because participants saw a benefit for themselves as well as the other members, there were "incentives for every member to work on the same problems" (p. 434). This clearly was also a goal across all three sites. They all sought to involve schoolteachers in the preparation of preservice teachers for work in classrooms. It was felt at all three sites that more careful collaboration with and between preservice and inservice teachers would make everyone's professional life better.

The second goal was the development of products and processes that could be refined, where "improved versions are publicly offered and eagerly received by all members as even better solutions" (p. 434). Indeed that is what the contributors to this book have done. They sought to devise a process, test it, improve it over time, and then share their work with a larger public, in the hope of its adoption or of additional testing and refinement by a new group of stakeholders.

The third goal was for institutions to conduct small tests of small changes. This featured "the frequent collection of small amounts of data—just enough data to tell whether the change has promise [that would] decrease resistance to change as the consequences and changes are smaller" (p. 435). A good example of this is the ongoing collection of information that UT–area teachers gathered and brought to planning meetings so that they could tweak the implementation of their alternative supervision model. Likewise, UA made notable shifts in its model's beginning years, and it continues to revisit small amounts of data for the purpose of honing their implementation, with teacher and faculty input and involvement.

Finally, the fourth goal was to arrive at solutions that embody "syntheses of knowledge located at different places in the system and represent better solutions than individual members or a single workgroup could produce alone" (p. 435). A good example of this was in Utah, where BYU students were able to work together and brainstorm multiple alternatives to classroom challenges, causing their classroom teachers to comment that more student teachers brought multiple perspectives and teaching techniques. What is important about this brainstorming process, which resulted in exponential growth, is what Morris and Hiebert (2009) call shared ownership:

> Changes in the process build on, rather than break, the social fabric already in place. Shared ownership of the product or process is the key to enlisting the users and local workgroups to construct and/or adapt the product and share what they learn. Conversely, respecting and using locally generated knowledge is the key to a sense of ownership. (p. 435).

## Failure

Although the work of Morris and Hiebert (2009) is helpful for describing what works right in a redesign effort, it also offers an explanation of why the UT model came to an untimely end. Since a critical component of redesign is what Morris and Hiebert called a shared goal, any significant shakeup in the constituents is likely to threaten the goal and therefore the model. When multiple participants left, new participants did not see the goal that was shared by their predecessors. For UT, the initial reform efforts relied too heavily on what Fullan et al. (1998) called the

> tremendous efforts . . . of small numbers of committed educators . . . [that can produce] nationwide reform programs . . . [that have] pockets of success. However, [these] school initiatives . . . [experience] stalled effects:
>
> 1. burnt-out teachers frustrated by the difficulty of, or lack of, progress;
> 2. problems in staying focused on, or clarifying, the vision in practice;
> 3. small groups of innovators being isolated from other educators in the school or school district—thus the failure to achieve whole school or whole district reform;
> 4. inability to disseminate the innovation on a wider scale without losing quality control. (p. 57)

Thus, the shifting vision of higher-level administrators at the school and university levels—including a new principal, a new role for Virginia as associate dean instead of Student Teaching Office coordinator, and a new faculty position at a different university for Adrian—resulted in teachers being deprived of their usual partners as well as an inability to disseminate reform to the larger network. As new faculty came in to fill the void, there was a loss of interest in dealing with newer problems and a desire to regress to the use of the traditional model at all sites.

## CONCLUSION

The attempts by BYU, UA, and UT faculty and teachers to devise an alternative supervision model are innovative, but they operate within a context that continues to be challenging. Despite these challenging contexts, some faculty at teacher preparation institutions remain determined to make a difference. These faculty need to know some of the realities that pioneers in reform have learned:

> What we know is, first, it is going to be a lot harder than we thought, and second, it will require some bold experiments that generate powerful forces,

> including, for example, teachers' energies and commitments unleashed by altered working conditions and new collective capacities, and students' intellectual labor in collaborating with other students to do the work of learning. (Fullan, 2007, p. 299)

The alternative supervision models described in this book represent a first step in the bold experiments calculated to unleash these powerful forces. In the following chapter, the next steps are discussed.

# CHAPTER 7

# Designing Future Models:
## Tailoring Alternatives to Fit Local Needs

*Adrian Rodgers and Deborah Bainer Jenkins*

I N CONSIDERING the limitations of traditional student teacher supervision and the literature that supports those approaches that we discussed in Chapters 1 and 2 of this book, and by examining three alternatives to traditional supervision described in Chapters 3, 4, and 5, readers have learned of the limitations and possibilities of quality supervision. Over the years, prominent educators have proposed the development of a carefully prepared cadre of teacher leaders capable of renewing teaching through careful work with student teachers. At the school level, as readers have learned, while cooperating teachers generally embrace the opportunity to work with preservice teachers, these teachers are frequently ill prepared for their role. They have unrealistic expectations and are reluctant to provide meaningful feedback to student teachers and evaluation for university supervisors. At the university level, reward systems disadvantage faculty members who take field supervision seriously. Cooperating teachers and university supervisors who are interested in supervision sometimes base their supervision practices on personal intuition and past experiences, which may or may not be relevant to the supervision task at hand. The data suggest that supervisors rarely draw upon basic knowledge of quality teaching practices when providing feedback to student teachers and that research-based knowledge of teacher education is largely absent from discussions about field-based practice among supervisors and with student teachers.

In this chapter our goal is to support readers who are stakeholders in student teacher supervision as they create and implement a reform agenda on supervision alternatives. To begin, we articulate the competencies that those involved in supervision need. We build on these competencies and suggest the knowledge, skills, and dispositions that supervisors need to develop. With such knowledge, skills, and dispositions in mind, we consider emerging trends for the future of how supervision is likely to be delivered, ranging from the elimination of traditional supervision options to distance supervision using technology. Our overall goal is to support supervision stakeholders in their empowering themselves, so we share tools that we have developed that are calculated to support faculty and school partners in their beginning to articulate partnership around the implementation of supervision alternatives. It is our hope that stakeholders will find these tools useful and will use them as they begin to envisage new, rich, and robust partnerships that promote the development of quality supervision. Ultimately, work on future supervision alternatives will need to be based in both research and an acknowledgment of public policy needs and wants, so we conclude the volume by offering recommendations for work that teams of teacher educators and school practitioners might undertake to begin to address these issues.

## BUILDING COMPETENCIES TO SUPPORT THE RECULTURING OF STUDENT TEACHER SUPERVISION

Over 25 years ago, Gleissman (1984) observed that the development of teaching skill is less about practice or experience and more a result of feedback, input, and support of others. Reiman and Thies-Sprinthall (1998) built on this claim, explaining that the "missing link" (p. 358) in teacher education reform is a "supervision and coaching culture" (p. 358) in schools and universities, where cadres of teachers and faculty members might engage in influential supervision and school-based action research to document success. This emphasis on a quality, customized relationship in which supervisors support teachers at the edge of learning through reflective dialogue is an alternative to role-taking without reflection, reflection without role-taking, short-term workshops, or an atmosphere that is exclusively supportive or exclusively challenging. It is widely recognized that becoming a teacher is a developmental process and that systematic observation and meaningful feedback are crucial to that process. Differentiated supervision, rooted in background knowledge of relevant theory and research, is also vital. Continuous, ongoing direction to engage in and then reflect on experience in a supportive yet challenging atmosphere leads to conceptual, problem-solving, and developmental growth.

In their seminal synthesis of teaching and research on teaching, Howey and Zimpher (1996) identified four types of essential teaching competences that can be developed in a supportive and challenging growth environment. These competencies suggest roles for supervisors if they are to facilitate student teacher development; in other words, the competencies tell us what works in preparing teachers. The first is *technical competence*, which includes mastery of instructional methods, requiring the supervisor to translate research and theory into applied practice. Therefore, supervisors must be knowledgeable of research, theory, and best practices. The second is *clinical competence*, which focuses on inquiry and models of teaching, requiring the supervisor to encourage reflection. To accomplish this, supervisors must be skilled in leading others to engage in analysis and reflective thinking. The third is *personal competence*, which involves self-understanding, with the supervisor creating a helpful and caring environment for addressing concerns. Thus, supervisors must be able to read and adapt their approach based on the individual and the situation. The fourth is *critical competence*, which focuses on moral autonomy and a commitment to social justice, requiring the supervisor to encourage divergent thinking, deep reflection, and dialogue on ethical issues in the classroom and the wider educational community. Therefore, supervisors must be current in their understanding and interpretation of educational events at the local, state, and national levels and must engage regularly in reflection and critical thinking themselves. While these supervisory roles sound daunting, experienced educators can perform them with a high degree of competence if they are appropriately prepared (Reiman & Thies-Sprinthall, 1998).

## ESSENTIAL KNOWLEDGE, SKILLS, AND DISPOSITIONS FOR SUPERVISORS

The National Council for Accreditation of Teacher Education and many teacher educators think about teacher preparation in terms of the knowledge, skills, and dispositions teachers need to be effective. In simplest terms and as a working definition, *knowledge* might be considered the theoretical and practical understanding of what is taught, how it might be taught, and how learners learn. *Skill* is the ability to put knowledge into action, and *disposition* is the willingness to adopt approaches relevant to learner needs. When these concepts are used in teacher education, two levels, or planes, of understanding must be considered. First, supervisors should have knowledge, skills, and dispositions that exceed those of the student teachers with whom they work. In other words, the supervisor needs to know how to teach children, be able to do it, and have the dispositions regarding child learning that we would expect of an accomplished teacher. Supervisors also need a second set of knowledge, skills, and dispositions; they must know how to supervise, be able to implement quality supervision strategies in practice, and have the dispositions appropriate to the preparation of beginning teachers.

To further illustrate this we offer the fictional case of Shelby, a first-grade student teacher, and Powell, her university supervisor. We'll discuss the knowledge, skills, and dispositions that Powell and Shelby need for teaching first graders, as well as the knowledge, skills, and dispositions Powell needs as Shelby's university supervisor. Although the learning curve for student teachers has never been a smooth one, teacher educators have learned a lot about teaching since the 1960s. Our goal in the next section is to revisit what we know about teaching and supervision and then propose future first steps in the redesign process.

## Knowledge of Effective Instruction

Although Shelby teaches small children, she and Powell need to know a lot. She needs to know multiple content areas, including social studies, mathematics, science, and language arts, and perhaps additional content areas such as music or art. Even within the discipline of language arts, she needs to know which children's literature options are appealing to her students, what writing they might undertake both independently and with peer or teacher assistance, and which dramatic activities are appropriate. She needs to know the theoretical base of how children learn generally, as depicted by Vygotsky (1962), Piaget (Piaget & Inhelder, 1969) and Gardner (1993). Since Shelby and Powell are involved with the development of motor skills in children, they would know about Gentile's (2000) taxonomy. Beyond having an understanding of learning theories, they would understand theories about the reading process and could draw on the theoretical work of Clay (1991) and the embedded theory or practitioner applications of Fountas and Pinnell (1996). Since Shelby is a beginning teacher, likely to misunderstand and misinterpret some knowledge, Powell needs to know more than Shelby. Most important, Powell's knowledge needs to be reasonably recent, since new children's books are written all the time, and newer books might be more relevant than older ones for particular lessons. Powell will have read Vygotsky, whereas Shelby most likely will have read about him. What is important here is that readers understand how complex the knowledge base is for first-grade teaching. In this hypothetical example we have glossed over just some of the basic knowledge a first-grade teacher needs for only one of the four or five content areas he or she teaches, and we explained how the supervisor needs to know a little more—or at least enough to sort out the misunderstandings of a beginning teacher.

Although in this example the knowledge required of a beginning teacher seems definable, defining good teaching has been a focus of research for over a century (see Cruickshank & Haefele, 2001, for an expanded discussion). In the mid-1960s, research attempted to link effective teaching to receiving high ratings from administrators, but the results were disappointing. Personality traits that were traditionally thought to be essential for effective teaching were not consistently linked to the ratings that teachers received. Even more disturbing was an influential study that examined the differences between schooling opportunities and learning outcomes for Black children and White children (Coleman, Campbell, Wood, Weinfeld, & York, 1966). The researchers found that differences in student achievement were largely associated with the socioeconomic status of the students and the community in which the school was located. Because the study found a significant impact on learning for socioeconomic variables but a lesser impact for the teacher and schooling influence, researchers began to more intensively investigate how teacher impacts could be maximized.

Over the past six decades, our knowledge of how teachers can provide effective instruction expanded greatly because of Coleman and his colleagues. In 1971, Rosenshine and Furst (1971) admitted in their meta-analysis of the characteristics of effective teachers that "we know very little about the relationship between classroom behavior and student gains" (p. 37), and called for more research on teaching. They found that effective teachers are those who provide clear instruction, use a variety of instructional strategies, are enthusiastic, keep students on task, and provide time and opportunity for students to learn the requisite material. There are lots of good research-based understandings of what effective teachers do, rooted in earlier research. Widely cited is a decade of video-based research on classroom management by Kounin (1977) that identified strategies effective teachers use to monitor students and to hold them accountable for their behavior and learning throughout the school year. Kounin described effective teachers as managing their classrooms by being aware of what is happening in all its corners (which he termed "withitness"), monitoring concurrent activities, presenting lessons at a brisk pace without interruptions, gaining and maintaining students' attention, and holding them accountable for learning throughout the lesson. Wilen and Clegg (1986) and LeNoir (1993) considered the use of questions in classrooms. They found questions needed careful wording that addressed both lower- and higher-order learning. Research on wait time—the length of time a teacher waits between posing a question and calling on a student to respond, then again before responding or reacting to the student's answer—shows that these pauses produces important outcomes: student responses are longer, more thorough, and at a higher cognitive level; more students volunteer; students are more confident in their responses; and positive interactions between students and the teacher increase (Berliner, 1987; Rowe, 1987; Tobin, 1987).

After 40 years of teacher research we know a lot about components of teaching that are relevant to all teachers regardless of the grade level or content area they teach. More recent research has begun to focus on highly situated teacher knowledge based in a particular content area or grade level. Clay (2005), for example, suggests how Shelby and other teachers of young children can tutor children who are having difficulty in learning to read. Bryk (Bryk, Biancarosa, Atteberry, Hough, & Dexter, 2008) has used complex tools to consider the effectiveness of primary-grade teachers within a complex professional development system known as the Literacy Collaborative, a system that includes a supervision component by a specially trained, school-level individual known as the literacy coordinator. In summary, then, much is known about what teachers need to know, and there is more evidence about the highly situated nature of teacher knowledge which is described in recent publications.

This knowledge base has significant implications for the future of supervision. Powell needs to know not only the historical research base that supports teacher knowledge, but also the emerging research base for what teachers need to know. This suggests that teacher educators and cooperating teachers who want to articulate the future of supervision need to identify supervisors who either have taken recent university course work, have attended research conferences, or have engaged in independent study or school-university partnership in which recent innovations and knowledge are likely to be discussed. Only in this way are supervisors likely to remain current with the field. It also suggests that it may be impossible for any one supervisor to stay current and that there might be merit in having supervisors and cooperating teachers with different interests and expertise share what they know periodically in some organized way. In this way, each person can have a sense of the continually changing knowledge base of what teachers need to know.

In addition to everything Shelby needs to know, Powell needs a knowledge base that supports supervision. It would help, for example, if he were familiar with the historical development of supervision and the alternatives to traditional approaches that we have described in this book. But there is much more that Powell needs to know. For example, we have heard many supervisors erroneously claim that student teachers are "just like the kids," meaning that the issues faced in the teaching of children are the same as those faced in the teaching of student teachers, who are adult learners. At face value this claim may bring a knowing nod from many supervisors, but when readers interrogate it they will acknowledge that adult learners are clearly different. One challenge is that adult learners, even those who are student teachers, have already have had years of significant teaching experiences. They've been students themselves for over a decade; they've taught Sunday school, nursery school, or Girl Scouts; they've observed and taught perhaps as a part of earlier field experiences or, for emergency credentialed teachers, are already teaching in their own classrooms; and most important, they have experienced considerable success and considerable failure as a part of this life experience. For these reasons, adult learners have significantly more experience than a child learner and so are likely to interpret supervisor comments in a more complex way.

A second factor in adult learning is the role of emotion. In writing about child learning and brain research, Lyons (1999) has focused on the role of the reticular activating system (RAS), the part of the brain that encodes emotional stamps on sensory input. Lyons explains:

> Feeling successful is critical in keeping the RAS open. The RAS must be opened and aroused in order for the child to attend; without attention the child cannot learn. Having a positive, nonthreatening, non-stressful experience while learning enhances the child's opportunity for success. (p. 78)

Just as this is true of child learning, it certainly applies to adult learners, who have a lot more at stake, especially if they are or perceive they are struggling in learning to teach. As supervisors we know that some lessons may go badly; it does not take too much for Shelby to find herself in tears. She has a lot on the line. She may be thousands of dollars in debt, face significant pressures at home, and feel a desperate need to successfully complete student teaching. Indeed, she is attempting to complete a degree that has less value for other career paths than many bachelor's degrees might. For these reasons, Shelby is under huge pressure to be successful. Ironically, her pressures and the role of the RAS mean that precisely when she needs to be at the top of her game in teaching and in debriefing with the supervisor, she is least likely to concentrate on constructive suggestions, because she is highly emotional. For Dirkx (2001), the literature on adult learning suggests that "emotion and feelings are deeply intertwined with perceiving and processing information from our external environments, storing and retrieving information in memory, reasoning, and the embodiment of learning" (p. 68).

Historically, teacher educators have considered the significance of developmental and adult learning perspectives. Frances Fuller (1969) recognized that the emotions of student teachers are as important as their thoughts or ideas. Her research found that most student teachers and novice teachers experience a similar sequence of phases in their personal growth: first, self-concerns; then, management or task concerns; finally, impact concerns (related to students, colleagues, and curriculum). Fuller's work demonstrates that student teachers have an abundance of personal and management concerns and need help managing the normal stress related to these concerns. Supervisors need to know the action steps to take and how to conference with student teachers based on the student teachers' level or stage of concern. With student teachers who have self-concerns, supervisors should provide information, clarify expectations and reasons for what the student teacher is expected to do, and describe how the expectations and responsibilities will affect the student teacher. Active listening and organizing support groups are especially appropriate when working with student teachers at this level of concerns. Student teachers at the next stage experience management concerns. They need specific, concrete management tips. They benefit from observing a teacher with strong management skills, collecting data during that observation, and engaging in a follow-up discussion to fully understand how the effective teacher made management decisions. We will revisit the impact of Fuller's work in the dispositions section of this chapter.

Powell will also need to have some understanding of the stance he will want to adopt in working with Shelby. The term *stance* is not typically used in the supervision literature, but is more commonly employed in the emerging literature on coaching that deals with expert practitioners supporting the development of experienced and veteran teachers. To borrow from this literature (Rodgers & Rodgers, 2007), then, supervisors have multiple options, including a directorial stance ("Teach it this way"), an open-ended stance ("Let me know if you have problems and I will help"), a mentor stance ("Here's how we do it here," "What would you like to do," "How can I help"), or a co-inquirer stance ("Let's learn about this together"). Powell might also consider how he might shift stance depending on his goal. To correct errors of procedure, he might be directorial ("Your administration of the standardized assessment was incorrect. Here is how to do it"), while to support student teacher growth, he might be a co-inquirer ("Let's think together about other possible ways of teaching this lesson").

Since there clearly is a knowledge base that is unique to the supervisor and cooperating teacher roles, quality supervisors will likely have taken either university course work in supervision or attended research conferences such as those sponsored by the Association of Teacher Educators, the Association for Supervision and Curriculum Development or the American Association of Colleges of Teacher Education. As with teacher knowledge, it is probably impossible for any one supervisor to stay current with knowledge on supervision, so there might be merit in having supervisors and cooperating teachers with different interests and expertise share what they know. If supervisors were to use what they know about supervision, they would likely seek to incite some excitement by the student teacher if only to arouse the RAS, but would work to avoid anguish and tears, since the student teacher cannot learn well in this state. Supervisors would likely focus on shorter, targeted debriefings, with a rough guideline being 20 minutes. Most important, after particularly challenging lessons or when the student teacher seems upset, it may be best to defer debriefing so that the student teacher can make sense of the event prior to conferencing with the supervisor.

Clearly, the current political and social climate focuses on holding teachers accountable for being effective—that is, for helping students learn content in ways that can be measured by high-stakes tests, student promotion, and graduation rates. Substantial research tells us what teachers need to do to bring about learning, and emerging research suggests what supervisors need to know to help beginning teachers.

## Skill in Teaching and Supervision

Beyond possessing the knowledge that first-grade teachers need, both Shelby and Powell need to be able to transform that knowledge into action. Since supervisors seldom model for student teachers, Powell does not need to be extremely skillful, but he certainly needs to know enough about classroom procedures to understand whether and why Shelby may have made a mistake and how it might be fixed. Cooperating teachers, on the other hand, need to be very skilled at classroom procedures, since they are constantly modeling for student teachers. A good hypothetical example of a skill is Shelby's ability to teach a mini-lesson. By definition, a minilesson is a lesson component with a specific lesson plan objective (for example, capitalizing names), generally limited in time (perhaps 10–20 minutes), and targeted only to those students having difficulty with the task (from one student to a whole group). If Shelby were to tackle capitals and commas in 40 minutes with the entire class, even though many students already understand capitalization rules, then she would have failed in teaching a quality minilesson. For this reason, Powell needs to be able to understand the source of Shelby's confusion, and Shelby's cooperating teacher would need to be able to execute multiple minilessons so that Shelby would have a model that she could emulate. While this example may seem straightforward, even as a beginning teacher Shelby would be expected to lead eight different reading and writing components for her students, consisting of multiple procedures, supports, and materials (for an example, see Fountas & Pinnell, 1996, pp. 27–28). Likewise, Powell would need to understand the intricacies of these procedures, and the co-operating teacher would be expected to execute quality modeling of them. For these reasons, and because teaching strategies are highly situated in contexts and grade levels, supervisors need to have considerable teaching skill at similar grade levels to the grade and content being supervised if they are to provide meaningful and insightful feedback to student teachers. Supervisors with recent teaching experience, ongoing contact with school classrooms, or participation in high-quality professional development are those likely to have this kind of teaching skill.

In addition to having teaching skill, Powell needs to develop his skills as a supervisor. That is, he needs to be able to put into action what he knows about the supervision process. To do this, seeking external supports through training or protocols can be helpful. Many turn to the work on cognitive coaching conducted by Costa and Garmston (1994), but there are other techniques. such as the Pathwise Classroom Observation System, that use observation tools (Educational Testing Service, 2002). Supervisors need to be skilled in determining what information to gather and how to gather it. One option is to use open-ended qualitative tools that gather a lot of information. Such tools include videotaping, audio-recording, narrative observations, focused questionnaires, and scripting in order. A second option is to use more focused quantitative tools as a part of focused observation. These tools include categorical frequency counts, visual diagrams such as sociograms, rating scales, or event or time-dependent systems. Numerous time-tested tools are available for use; they include the Flanders Interaction Analysis System (Flanders, 1970), used to code teacher talk and student talk at 3- to 5-second intervals throughout the lesson, and the Qualitative Measures of Teaching Performance Scale (Rink & Werner, cited in Darst, Zakrajsek, & Mancini, 1989), designed to collect data simultaneously on the type of teaching task, task presentation, student responses, and teacher feedback. Some classic instruments have been updated and modified for use in specific content areas, such as the Academic Learning Time-Physical Education (Siedentop, Tousignant, & Parker, 1982), modified to measure the portion of time in a physical education lesson that a student is involved in motor activity at an appropriate success rate.

In addition to these specific instruments, supervisors need to master communication and observation skills to implement conferences and observations that are meaningful and timely. This is in direct contrast to the intuitive approach that researchers say is used by most supervisors, in which conclusions are drawn without specific data and conferences are characterized by the supervisor talking, evaluating, or even criticizing while the student teacher listens passively. Effective supervision requires training and preparation on the part of both the teacher education program and the supervisors they select to fill this pivotal role in transforming student teachers into effective practitioners.

While supervision practice should vary depending on the model espoused by the teacher education program, basic skills characterize most supervision models. For example, the need for establishing a helpful and trusting relationship with the student teacher is vital at the beginning of the field experience. This includes becoming acquainted; establishing roles, expectations, and preferred ways of communicating; and clarifying how supervision is implemented. When the developmental model is applied, for example, this initial phase is expanded to discuss learning styles, personal understandings of teaching, self-analysis, and developmental goals. When applying clinical supervision, discussion about observations, data collecting, and analysis of teaching might receive more emphasis.

Foundational to effective supervision is the background work of teacher education programs to identify and articulate the theoretical and philosophical underpinnings of their supervision efforts. The supervision model or approach the program advocates determines the role of the supervisors, the skills they will need to master, and the outcomes they seek to build in student teachers. For example, *clinical supervision* is a form of democratic inquiry that encourages teachers to consider alternatives, to solve problems, and to think about their teaching behaviors based on their meaning and structure in teaching events. In clinical supervision, the supervisor is a "humble questioner" who understands the unpredictability of classroom events and recognizes that there are no absolutes in teaching, but rather, that teaching and learning is "a process of successive approximations" (Reiman & Thies-Sprinthall, 1998, p. 177). In contrast, *developmental supervision* aims at refining and expanding the teacher's instructional repertoire through a carefully designed support program attuned to the individual's learning and developmental needs. Developmental supervision assumes an ethical responsibility for going beyond instructional changes to promoting the teacher's cognitive development and growth, requiring the supervisor to be able to continually read the student teacher and to adjust the supervision process to stimulate development. Thus, it is important in rethinking supervision that teacher educators give a lot of consideration, not only to how supervisors have prepared and the skills they need to have, but also to the theoretical underpinnings on which supervision and teacher preparation rest. Structured opportunities must be provided for supervisors to identify, discuss, and explore these assumptions with the goal of crafting more potent forms of providing feedback and growth opportunities for student teachers.

Across supervision approaches, supervisors also need skills in observing and conducting conferences. According to Rink (in press), observation is an essential skill for collecting information on the teaching-learning process and enables assessment of the teaching process and the performance of the teacher. Supervisors, then, should be knowledgeable about and skilled in the use of observation to gain knowledge of teaching: specifically, collecting data during observation that is valid and reliable, interpreting that data in ways that are meaningful for instruction, and conferencing with student teachers to use the information to make changes in their teaching and instructional practice. In the preobservation conference, the supervisor needs to learn the objective, focus, and procedures the student teacher plans for the lesson. During the observation, the supervisor gathers as much information as possible about the teaching episode and student responsiveness, being careful to record legible data without judging for use in the postconference. The postobservation conference, ideally conducted immediately after the lesson, requires the supervisor to pose reflective questions, then to actively listen to the student teacher. The goal here is to avoid the initiate-respond-evaluate sequences that have been so aptly critiqued by Cazden (1983, 1986) in favor of questions that will solicit information from the student teacher and support the co-construction of understanding in the student teacher's lesson choices. Adrian has written about the importance of asking better questions in *The Effective Literacy Coach* (Rodgers & Rodgers, 2007), but these kinds of questions begin to go a long way toward a developmental approach:

- Tell me about the lesson.
- Did you accomplish your objectives?
- What do you think worked particularly well?
- What changes, if any, would you make in the lesson?
- What teacher behavior should we focus on to develop and refine in the next observation?

As reflectivity and trust develops, the supervisor could try the following questions, which are more calculated to support deeper levels of reflection:

- What is it that you wonder about this lesson?
- What is a challenge you faced in planning/teaching this lesson?
- What is a counterexample?
- In rethinking what you just said, tell me about _____.

- On the one hand, you said _____, but on the other hand, what about _____?
- As you deliberate about _____, tell me what you are thinking about _____.
- Tell me more about that.

Following this active listening, most approaches prescribe further probes and comments from the supervisor, focused on understanding the student teacher's thinking and decision making related to the lesson and on pointing out links to research and best practices that relate to the lesson. Setting goals or structuring the next observation concludes the postobservation conference.

Teacher educators have begun to build the skills of experienced teachers through the development of mentor programs for 1st-year teachers (Moir, 2003) and coaching models for more experienced teachers (Rodgers & Rodgers, 2007). Even at the time of writing, a number of faculty at The Ohio State University are emulating the research done on micro*teaching* at Stanford in the 1960s and 1970s to collaborate on the development of video protocols to support coaching. Adrian is collaborating with Emily Rodgers on protocols for the development of micro*coaching*. Patricia Scharer and Gay Su Pinnell are collaborating with Anthony Bryk and Irene Fountas on the collection of video samples illustrating innovative literacy teaching to be used in coaching settings (Walker, Sawyers, Scharer, & Fountas, 2008). Belinda Gimbert and her collaborators are piloting online video streaming for teachers, prepared through alternative routes, for use in coaching contexts. Through their Project KNOTtT (Kansas, Nevada, Ohio, and Texas Transition to Teaching), designed to strengthen systems' capacity collaboratively, university- and school-based teacher educators offer e-coaching to beginning teachers who seek teacher credentials through innovative alternative pathways. These new teachers participate in an online learning community and experience coaching in the content areas of mathematics, science, special education, and principles of learning and teaching. Embedded in this online learning forum are virtual coaching classrooms that are supported by a Web-based platform called Live Meeting. Within the coaching process, video streaming affords novice teachers exposure to best teaching practices that are modeled by master teachers. This process accelerates the development of these novice teachers' pedagogical content knowledge. With this body of work currently in development, it is likely that teacher educators will soon be publishing the results of their work on the use of video in the skill development of preservice and in-service teachers.

## Dispositions of Student Teachers and Supervisors

Besides knowledge and skills, Shelby and Powell both need the disposition to be early childhood educators, and Powell needs the disposition to be a quality supervisor. In the United States, the dispositions for early childhood educators have been identified by the National Association for the Education of Young Children (www.naeyc.org). They include being respectful of other cultures and having a willingness to work with parents. Clearly, then, Powell would need to be sufficiently disposed to support Shelby in working with parents, and if he had some expertise in this disposition, he might even share with Shelby the usefulness of authors such as Sudia McCaleb (1995), who has written about how teachers might work with parents from multiple cultures.

In addition to the dispositions one might expect of preservice teachers, supervisors need dispositions related to their supervisor role. Sprinthall has built on Piaget's work with children's intellectual growth and proposed five conditions for adult psychological growth and development: role-taking, reflection, balance, continuity, and a balance of support and challenge (see Reiman & Thies-Sprinthall, 1998; Thies-Sprinthall, 1984; or Sprinthall, Reiman, & Thies-Sprinthall, 1993, for a fuller discussion). Sprinthall proposes that adults learn through interaction with their environment. As individuals go through the equilibration (or balancing) process to assimilate and internalize new information and experiences, they gradually develop more complex cognitive structures, enabling better decision making and problem solving. Sprinthall explained that the feelings associated with new learning must be worked through during the equilibration process through relaxed reflection. Thus, it is important in the supervisory context that supervisors be disposed to engaging the student teacher in interactive talk. Since group dialogue—such as what might be encountered in the student teaching seminar—provides different perspectives, it is important that the supervisor be disposed to support opportunities for additional enlightenment and personal and professional growth.

Vygotsky (1962) supported the idea that formal and informal discussions are basic to cognitive growth and conceptual understanding. He has described the importance of the zone of proximal development, a concept appropriated by Wood, Bruner, and Ross (1976), who coined the term *scaffolding* to describe the support a knowledgeable other provides to a learner. As Rodgers and Rodgers (2004) have described previously,

> the analogy of a scaffold is a useful one because it describes the process [by which the knowledgeable other and the learner interact as the] learner moves

toward independence. A worker constructs a scaffold to work on an area of a building that is out of reach. The scaffold is only temporary and is removed when the work is finished. It can be put together and taken down quickly, as the need for assistance arises. (p. 2)

This suggests that supervisors need to be disposed to help student teachers not just generally, but at specific points of difficulty and in highly customized ways that are unique to each student teacher and that will change over time. Specifically, the opportunities built into the student teaching experience should provide a realistic challenge to that student teacher, and the discussion and questions posed by the supervisor should model slightly more complex thinking to maximally stimulate growth.

In the section above where we considered supervisor knowledge, we discussed the work of Frances Fuller (1969), who took a developmental perspective toward supervision. Many teacher educators have used this concept to develop programs aimed at supporting dispositional growth around supervision. For example, Hunt (1976) suggested that supervisors needed to be disposed to "read and flex" (p. 269) or adapt their approach to the needs of the student teacher based, in part, on Fuller's stages of concern. Student teachers with basic, personal, and management concerns need more structure from supervisors. Supervisors need to focus on concrete behaviors, actions, and concepts as they have dialogue with or question these student teachers. Feedback to these student teachers needs to be given frequently and should be specific, even outlining specific steps or tasks to be taken. As student teachers move to higher stages of concern, the supervisor should provide less structured observation and interaction. Supervisors can focus on abstract concepts and ideas related to teaching, and questions can relate to broader educational issues, theory, and ethics. Feedback should emphasize self-critiquing, with the supervisor providing a general discussion of teaching events or tasks observed rather than specific, isolated incidents.

A conceptual understanding of human development and its application to teacher development enable effective supervision across supervisory configurations and models, but supervisors need to be disposed to and willing to make such customizations. We suggest that teacher education programs ensure that they and their supervisors understand the implications of developmental theory and research for how they structure and implement field experiences. While supervisors intuitively tend to apply helping behaviors when working with students, a fuller understanding of this important work will enable them to perform their supervisory responsibilities more thoughtfully and effectively. Further, this knowledge suggests that the format of the traditional student teaching seminar, usually an evening class taken concurrently with student teaching, should be revisited. While these seminars are intended to reduce stress related to student teaching, too often they focus on career planning, developing résumés, and practicing for interviews. We suggest that this time would be more helpful for student teachers if the sessions were structured around Fuller's concerns model, with the intent of defusing the anxiety experienced by all student teachers and guiding them through reflection and discussion that results in personal and professional growth.

## THE FUTURE DIRECTION OF ALTERNATIVE DELIVERY OPTIONS IN STUDENT TEACHER SUPERVISION

Increasingly, prospective teachers and school districts see themselves as consumers of higher education and some colleges in the United States have begun to take an increasingly market-oriented approach to delivering teacher preparation. A part of this adaptation to the changing marketplace is the creation of courses on demand and distance or alternative-delivery options for course work and field experience. Adrian's first experiences with distance education was in the early 1980s when faculty at the Memorial University of Newfoundland were pioneering correspondence courses, video courses, telecourses featuring video or voice links, alternative site delivery featuring course delivery both in multiple communities and in community settings such as schools, and hybrid options featuring components of multiple alternatives. With the rise of the Web, high-speed connections, online library holdings, inexpensive computers, commonplace video technology, podcasts, online social networks such as Facebook, and online video conferencing such as Skype, teacher educators involved in initial and ongoing teacher credential programs now have more delivery options than ever before. We think future technology applications will range widely, encompassing the entire abandonment of traditional teacher preparation, the increased use of technology in teacher preparation, the continued emergence of online-only preparation, and the more sophisticated use of technology in supervision.

### Abandonment of Traditional Teacher Preparation

At the time of this writing, different states in the United States are experimenting with alternatives to traditional teacher preparation. In Adrian's home state of Ohio, individuals with any bachelor's degree can receive a temporary license that permits them to teach; they can then enroll part time in the same university course work that a traditional candidate seeking licensure would take to receive renewals on the initial license. Essentially, in Ohio this is an on-the-job-training approach to teacher preparation. At the time of writing the Ohio governor has proposed an intriguing alternative to traditional teacher preparation: the deconstruction of what Kennedy (1999) called the role of preservice teacher education (see www.aces.k12 .oh.us/Jefferson%20engagement%20and%20new%20schools/January %2028%20governor%27s%20state%20of%state%20address.pdf). The governor and his supporters see this as an innovation based on potent forms of job-embedded professional development. Although such innovations are significant in the redesign process, they do place an even greater emphasis on the significance of the role of supervisors in supporting novice teachers.

Whether or not the Ohio governor's plans are realized, in the future we expect increased interest from policy makers in shortening traditional teacher preparation programs; in implementing greater accountability measures such as teacher tests, standardized student tests, and school or district report cards; and in relying on alternative teacher preparation and alternative schools such as charter schools to bring forth innovation. At the same time, we see these efforts as inadvertently defeating innovation efforts. While state governments could previously partner with teacher preparation institutions when a few colleges of education were doing the bulk of the teacher preparation, alternative teacher preparation models make it difficult to partner with anyone. While state departments of education could partner with large districts in academic emergency to make needed improvements, they are unlikely to partner with failing charter schools, since it is difficult for something the size of a state department of education to partner with one particular school. In some states charter schools go largely unmonitored, because enrolled students do not take the same accountability tests that public school students do. In other words, marketplace pressures to offer highly customized teacher preparation will make it difficult to hold any particular entity responsible for quality control; this will increase the reliance on easily administered, relatively cheap pencil-and-paper teacher tests.

Another interesting thing may happen because of market pressures and despite public policy intervention. Regardless of how policy makers act, many schools and school districts may continue to demand and exclusively hire teachers prepared in traditional teacher preparation programs. If this comes to pass, it will be because those who are hiring believe in the way they were prepared and want beginning teachers to have been prepared in the same way. Just because increasing numbers of prospective teachers may take alternative licensure options and become credentialed teachers, this may not lead to employment. In fact, it may be that science, mathematics, and English as a second language teachers will increasingly come through expedited, alternative preparation because of the demand in those fields, whereas employers may continue to demand that teachers in other areas complete a more conventional teacher preparation path.

## Technology and Online Options in Teacher Preparation and Supervision

Although it is difficult to say what the future holds for the role of public policy in initial teacher preparation, the literature offers teacher educators more insight into how technology might mediate teacher preparation and supervision. One popular option is the use of technology tools such as Taskstream (www.Taskstream.com) or Teachscape (www.Teachscape .com) as an online component to an already existing course. Through the use of such tools, student teachers can share readings, reflections, student work, and videos with peers, supervisors, and cooperating teachers. A second direction in teacher preparation is the adoption by the National Council for Accreditation of Teacher Education (NCATE) accredited or regionally accredited bricks-and-mortar colleges of education of increased online degree options. Indeed, only a few years ago, the University of Phoenix and Nova Southeastern University were the recognized online options, but in 2009 the highly regarded *U.S. News and World Report* special edition on America's best graduate schools listed 20 institutions offering online graduate options, including a number of well-recognized state and private institutions ("The Largest Online Grad Programs," 2009). Interestingly, these and other online institutions have different missions, ranging from those of state universities such as the University of Illinois at Urbana-Champaign, to those of religiously affiliated institutions such as the University of Dayton, to those of publicly traded institutions such as Grand Canyon University. Another option is the abandonment of the bricks-and-mortar option in favor of an online-only approach. Although teacher educators and prospective students of such programs are understandably cautious of these options, in November 2006 Western Governors University received the "first ever NCATE accreditation for an online institution" (Castaldi, 2006, p. 1). While it is likely that online-only options will continue to be received by the marketplace of consumers and credential experts with caution, the considerable weight of NCATE accreditation will play an important role in the continued legitimization of online teacher preparation.

Teacher educators have been writing for some time about how technology can be used for supervision, and we found the review offered by

Simpson (2006) to be most comprehensive. She reported that distance supervision options are useful when an institution is placing students in the field over a large geographic area or in a remote area with limited infrastructure or because the university does not supply a university supervisor. In these situations, distance options provide ongoing support between faculty at the university and the cooperating teacher and student teacher in the field. In some of these situations a local university supervisor is hired, and in others the cooperating teacher and university faculty fulfill the supervisor role. Although Simpson's work was recently published, she noted that most research on field experience in distance-delivered initial teacher preparation programs was conducted in the mid-1990s. Since the use of video at that time was still complicated by technological issues, a number of the studies she described focus on the use of e-mail and secured Web sites as ways to support field students. The work of Wittenburg and McBride (1998) and Laffey and Musser (1998) was certainly cutting edge at the time, but it has now entered the technological mainstream.

Much more cutting edge is the work of Broadley (2000), who used video recordings to augment printed and audiotaped recordings, and Garrett and Dudt (1998), who used live video supervision. According to Simpson (2006), Broadley was involved in a collaboration with Guyanan schools and used videotape clips to supplement other artifacts from the field. This led Simpson to conclude that "a strong focus may be kept on reflection and dialogue while partially replacing personal visiting time by other means of assessment" (p. 247). In terms of technology purchases, Garrett and Dudt's use of synchronous videoconferencing was more ambitious and required the support of a federal grant. Using these funds, they established three sites throughout western Pennsylvania and equipped each with multiple video cameras, live remote videoconferencing facilities, and the transmission of two-way video and audio signals between the sites using an ISDN line, which transmits data at about 50 times the rate of a conventional telephone cable. Supervisors at the university then conferenced with cooperating teachers and student teachers in remote field sites and observed lessons. Garrett and Dudt used multiple measures focused on the mediated component of supervision, but they reported results not much different from what teacher educators would expect with real-time supervision. Although this was an impressive technological feat for rural Pennsylvania in the late 1990s, high-speed data lines are now increasingly popular throughout the United States. This suggests that live observation of preservice teachers by university supervisors off site might be possible at much lower cost than the costs incurred by Garret and Dudt. Although costs might be lower, using video to supervise preservice teachers over a distance still requires considerable resources such as multiple video cameras, high-speed transmission lines, and technical support. For these reasons, faculty who might want to supervise from a distance using technology will still need to collaborate with technicians and may require a memorandum of understanding between the school and the university so that owner-ship and responsibilities for maintaining equipment are clearly understood.

## NEXT STEPS: USING TOOLS FOR FUTURE PLANNING

In this chapter we have proposed essential competencies for supervisors; considered the knowledge, skills, and dispositions that supervisors need; and painted a picture of the future by describing potential public policy decisions and technological trends in teacher education. But what does it all mean? And how does a small group of teacher educators at a medium-sized university embark on articulating a redesign of supervision? As faculty who have served on smaller and medium-sized campuses, we understand the challenges of the redesign process and the supportive environment of smaller settings unfettered by large bureaucracies. And for faculty serving at larger, research-intensive institutions, we understand the pressures posed by publication requirements and the intimacies offered by being responsible for a very select group of students. It certainly would be pos-sible for those interested in redesign to adopt one of the models discussed in Part II of this book, but most faculty will want to have some degree of customization, and may even want to embark on their own total redesign effort. To support and help faculty in moving forward with partial or com-plete redesign efforts, Adrian has devised a number of what he calls think-ing tools intended to support the thought process during the initial stages of planning a redesign effort.

We suggest that you use these tools as a group—with a small number of faculty who you think will direct the redesign process. We would sug-gest that if you need more than five faculty to be involved, you hold sepa-rate meetings limited to three or four faculty each. In any case, these instruments are calculated to work with a small number of faculty highly invested in redesign efforts. After an initial plan is formulated, drafts of an action plan might be presented to a larger group. We would also note that while it is never a good idea to plan a particular institutional initiative around particular individuals, it is a good idea to think about who will get the ball rolling on particular initiatives. In other words, in their early in-ception, creative alternatives to the status quo are highly reliant on par-ticular faculty or teachers with particular sets of skills. After that initial start-up phase, it is a good idea to devolve responsibility to multiple stake-holders so that no initiative relies on just one individual. Finally, we invite you to copy the thinking tools that follow and enlarge them on poster paper for your use in brainstorming sessions.

## Getting Started by Thinking About Resources

To get started, we begin with the "resource thinking tool" (see Figure 7.1). This tool is intended to help users consider the university and school assets that would support alternative student teacher supervision approaches, the needs of the teacher preparation unit, the stakes that each individual or group faces, and the challenges faced by each unit. We would propose that for each vacant square, users try to bullet two–four notes that respond to the prompts. We would also suggest that users begin at the top and bottom of the tool and work from the left and right edges toward the center. The following is a hypothetical example to explain how the tool might be completed.

Imagine faculty working at a medium-sized, religiously affiliated institution who have cultivated close partnerships with some parochial schools and some urban schools. Beginning in the upper-left corner of the tool, faculty might list under *University Assets/Structure* bullets like "highly responsive institution" and "good philanthropic support." *Under University Assets/ Culture* faculty might note "commitment to social justice" and "responsive administration." It should be noted that the concepts of structure and culture are borrowed from Fullan (2007). Reading this book may be helpful to users of the resource thinking tool. Users would then move to the bottom-left corner of the first column and might bullet for *University Challenges/Structure* a comment such as "cumbersome human resources & payroll." In the *University Challenges/Culture* box, users might bullet "resistance to teachers in faculty roles." Users might then move to the middle row, and for *Stakes/ What's in it for the university*, they might record "action on social justice." Faculty would then deliberate on their perception of the university's needs and might bullet in the *We Need* box comments such as "a clearly articulated action plan linking this redesign with social justice." Of course, response will vary depending on the institution, faculty, and stakeholder needs, and responses will be complex as users move to the far-right edge of the tool and then to the top and bottom, working toward the center. Nevertheless, the goal would be that when this tool is complete, users will have a good understanding of what they need to do (one of the center rows), what is at stake for multiple stakeholders (the other center row), and the structure and culture that has created those needs and stakes.

## Why Redesign?

The second step in initiating a reform effort is articulating why it should be undertaken. As more stakeholders learn of the proposed reform effort,

**Figure 7.1.** Resource thinking tool.

| | Group | University Assets | College of Education Assets | Faculty Assets | Student Teacher Assets | School Children Assets | Teacher Assets | School Assets | District Assets |
|---|---|---|---|---|---|---|---|---|---|
| **Assets** | *Structure* | | | | | | | | |
| | *Culture* | | | | | | | | |
| **We need** | | | | | | | | | |
| **Stakes/ What's in it for me?** | | | | | | | | | |
| | *Culture* | | | | | | | | |
| **Challenges** | *Structure* | | | | | | | | |
| | *Group* | University Challenges | College of Education Challenges | Faculty Challenges | Student Teacher Challenges | School Children Challenges | Teacher Challenges | School Challenges | District Challenges |

129

they are likely to ask the very reasonable question "Why do it?" To support the development of answers to this question, Adrian has designed a second thinking tool, provided in Figure 7.2, the "why do it? thinking tool." As readers learned in Chapter 1, Wilson and Daviss (1994) suggest four reasons for innovation, and each is listed in a box of Figure 7.2. Users should consider responses to each prompt and complete the eight boxes. After completion the right column should list compelling reasons for redesign; if it does not, faculty may want to reconsider their effort.

This is a fairly simple approach that will answer many who ask what is to be gained, but faculty could consider even more sophisticated analyses such as a consideration of the value added by a redesign. Even a basic book on personal finance offers explanations of risk such as *Default risk*, or the risk of an investment becoming worthless; *Event risk*, or the risk of the unexpected beyond the control of management; *Extension risk*, or the risk that the investment may not return what is expected when it is expected; and *Opportunity risk*, or the risk that the effort invested in one initiative will deprive investors of the opportunity to invest that same energy somewhere else (Edelman, 1998). Although these risks are in the financial marketplace, we think that they also apply surprisingly well to risk-benefit assessment involved in complex partnerships. Hopefully, faculty and school partners will enter into partnerships and redesign efforts with a careful appreciation of risks and benefits.

**Figure 7.2.** Why do it? thinking tool.

| *How does the current design . . .* | *How does the proposed design . . .* |
|---|---|
| . . . capitalize on success? | . . . capitalize on success? |
| . . . improve quality? | . . . improve quality? |
| . . . expand usefulness? | . . . expand usefulness? |
| . . . keep costs low? | . . . keep costs low? |

## Building on Needs to Action

The third tool, the "building on needs to action thinking tool," is illus-trated in Figure 7.3, and it is intended to support users in building on constituent needs to create action that will result in redesign efforts. To begin, users should copy the bullets recorded in the "we need" row of Figure 7.1 into the boxes on the periphery of Figure 7.3. Users would then complete the boxes with the caption "Current." In other words, users will want to record what they currently do, the time line for that work, the costs associated with it, and the individuals who complete the work. Users should note that there is some mismatch between what constituents need and what the institution does. This is because if everyone's needs were met, there would be no need for redesign. Users should then list alternative actions, the time line for that work, the costs that will be incurred, and the individuals who will do the work. After completing these boxes, users should note a closer match between what the constituents need and what the alternative redesign will accomplish.

## Developing an Action Plan

The final step is to develop an action plan. The "action plan thinking tool," Figure 7.4, is designed to accomplish that. The action plan has three sec-tions. In the first, key features of the redesign, users should list at the top of each column the names of the people who will do different work. This could be actual names of personnel or roles such as "faculty" or "dean." Under each name or role, users should then bullet what work each person will do. In the second section, "Buy-in Required," users list the high-level school and university personnel involved and what they will do. These boxes will include work that will be done by a district superintendent or delegate and a college of education dean or delegate. Users would then complete the boxes labeled "Middle Level/Schools" and "Middle Level/University." These boxes will contain tasks to be completed by principals and department chairs. Last, the "Ground Level/Schools" and "Ground Level/University" boxes will record work to be undertaken by teachers and faculty. The intent of this section is to ensure that all levels of school and university personnel have bought into the initiative. We recommend that if there is not some buy-in from every level of school and university, faculty should work to build buy-in before continuing. The third section is titled "Actions and Next Steps." In this section, users should list what they have to do to prepare to undertake the redesign, the initial steps of implementation, and what users will need to do to

**Figure 7.3.** Building on needs to action thinking tool.

| University WE NEED | Student Teachers WE NEED | | | District WE NEED |
|---|---|---|---|---|
| | **CURRENT INITIATIVES** | | | |
| | Initiatives: | Initiatives: | Initiatives: | |
| | Time Line: | Time Line: | Time Line: | |
| | Costs: | Costs: | Costs: | |
| College of Education WE NEED | People: | Activities: | | School WE NEED |
| | **ALTERNATIVE INITIATIVES** | | | |
| | Initiatives: | Initiatives: | Initiatives: | |
| | Time Line: | Time Line: | Time Line: | |
| | Costs: | Costs: | Costs: | |
| Faculty WE NEED | People: | Activities: | | Teachers WE NEED |
| | School Children WE NEED | | | |

**Figure 7.4.** Action plan thinking tool.

### I. Key Features of the Redesign

| Person/Role | Person/Role | Person/Role |
|---|---|---|
| Tasks | Tasks | Tasks |

### II. Buy-in Required

| **Level** | **Schools** | **University** |
|---|---|---|
| Highest | | |
| Middle | | |
| Ground | | |

### III. Actions and Next Steps

| |
|---|
| Preparing |
| Implementing |
| Assessment and Evaluation |

assess and evaluate their work. In the first chapter of this book, we discussed Fullan's (1993) concept of "ready-fire-aim" (p. 31), explaining that those interested in reform needed to get *ready* and *fire*, or get the ball rolling. As more information is collected, reformers could then *aim*, or increasingly tailor their efforts with the goal of success. The four figures included in this chapter are intended to support users as they undertake the *ready* phase of redesign.

## CONCLUSION

Despite the rise and decline of traditional teacher preparation programs over 5 decades, student teacher supervision remains largely unchanged. In the era of alternative teacher preparation and increased accountability, it is clearly time for teacher educators not only to consider alternatives, but also to pilot redesign efforts intended to tailor supervision around the very specific needs of an increasingly diverse pool of prospective teachers being prepared for increasingly diverse school settings. It is customary to conclude scholarly works with calls for research, but it must also be acknowledged that the shifting nature of public policy governing teacher preparation sometimes forces the hand of teacher educators before systematic research can be conducted. For this reason teacher educators will want to consider how they might conduct inquiry within politicized contexts and how they can operate within state mandates that increasingly constrain creativity in teacher preparation even as they inadvertently erode standards. At the same time, current evaluation of teacher preparation models tends to be limited to perceptions of the models, but it does not focus on features of student teacher performance such as lesson design, delivery, and classroom management. Rodgers, Kerbow, and Hung (2007) have begun to look at how expert assessors evaluate the teaching of veteran teachers, but the field remains wide open for how preservice teachers are evaluated and linked to student learning.

One possible result of state mandates may be the introduction of a double standard: teachers prepared in traditional preparation programs may be held to increasingly strict state standards while those prepared in alternative programs may have increasingly minimal requirements. Although this is a potential challenge for teacher educators, this double standard again illustrates the need for customizing supervision to meet the needs of different student teachers who are prepared in different ways. Alternative preparation models in which beginning teachers have to serve multiyear residencies will also pose challenges for traditional ways of thinking about supervision. It is possible that formative coaching activities conducted on the job will become blurred with summative supervision activities that may be a part of teacher retention and promotion. Given the shifting nature of teacher preparation, teacher educators and school partners will want to consider multiple supervision approaches to meet the needs of student teachers and those who support them.

# Glossary of Key Terms

These key terms refer to individuals, roles, stakeholders, and entities involved in supervision. Since terms vary across sites, states, and countries, this glossary is not intended to offer exhaustive definitions but to provide readers with a working understanding of how terms are used with the goal of soliciting discussion around the people and places involved in supervision.

**Students.** Children in schools.

**Emergency certified teacher** or **Provisional temporarily certified teacher.** An individual who is paid by a school or district to teach students but has not completed an accredited teacher licensure program. Emergency certification is more common in high-need schools or districts such as urban core areas or rural areas, or in high-need subject areas such as English as a second language, math, science, technology, or special education. The teacher with an emergency credential is often enrolled in a teacher preparation program and frequently seeks to have his or her daily teaching experiences serve as his or her field experiences. Thus an emergency certified teacher is similar to a preservice teacher in that he or she is still studying the fundamentals of teaching, but different from the preservice teacher because he or she is conducting university studies on the job and because the primary responsibility is teaching the children in his or her classrooms.

**Alternative licensed or certified teacher.** An individual who is paid by a school or district to teach students but has not completed a traditional pathway, such as a 4-year undergraduate or 1-year graduate degree. Alternative licensure is more common in high-need schools or districts, such as urban core areas or rural areas or in high-need subject areas. The teacher holding alternative licensure has completed a series of experiences certified by a state licensure agency as meeting teacher licensure requirements. Alternative licensure can mean different things in different states, because in some states alternatively licensed teachers are considered fully certified, while in other states they are not. In some states, alternative licensure might be obtained after completing something as minimal as one test. In other states, alternative licensure might be obtained after completing a complex set of requirements, possibly including the same requirements as a traditional credentialed teacher, only over a different time line, on the job, and perhaps from different institutions.

**Teacher education.** The courses, institutions, and faculty involved in teacher preparation. This includes the school, college, or department of education (SCDE), as well as affiliated colleges and faculty in arts and science involved in teacher preparation.

**Teacher educator** can have two different meanings. In its widest context, it is any individual at the college level involved in teacher education. More narrowly, it means core faculty in SCDEs who prepare teachers, such as methods faculty, foundations faculty, university supervisors, and faculty in doctoral programs in teacher education that study teacher preparation.

**Adjunct.** A faculty member paid per course or per student for work in teaching or supervising. Typically he or she holds at least a master's degree and often has school teaching experience. An adjunct may be teaching at schools by day and college by night or be retired from school teaching. This status is important in discussions of teacher preparation because individuals with adjunct status may be viewed by teacher educators as having marginal status.

**Tenured/Tenure track faculty.** Faculty members who have completed or are completing a rigorous internal review process by their college or university. These faculty would hold terminal degrees and must meet research, teaching, and service expectations. These faculty are often on *hard* money (funds allotted for positions in the university budget), whereas adjuncts are on *soft* money (funds paid by grants or from different budgetary lines that meet the needs of the SCDE). Therefore, tenured and tenure track faculty are often seen as more central to teacher preparation than adjuncts.

**Field placement coordinator.** An individual staff or faculty member at a university who identifies and recruits cooperating teachers to host preservice teachers. In some cases there may be many coordinators who place preservice teachers in addition to fulfilling faculty roles; in other cases, there is one coordinator who makes all placements; and still in other cases, there may be a student teaching office with multiple coordinators and a head of the office with considerable administrative authority.

**Provisional temporarily certified teacher.** *See* **Emergency certified teacher.**

**Student teachers and interns.** Preservice teachers near the end of their teacher preparation program and engaged in a final and intensive field experience. For student teachers this experience may be 10–15 weeks of 5-days-a-week teaching, where the individual has significant responsibility for planning, implementing, and evaluating lessons. In some cases the term *intern* is used interchangeably with *student teacher*, and in other settings, *intern* denotes a field experience student placed in one setting for 1 year, while *student teacher* denotes an individual in one setting for one semester. These interns may be completing a mid-level field experience in the fall or an intense student teaching experience in the spring.

**Mentors.** Often experienced teachers who guide teachers in their 1st year on the job.

**Novice/Beginning teacher.** An individual teacher in his or her first to third year on the job.

In addition to these individuals, there are settings described in this book that have very nuanced meanings.

**Public schools.** Schools almost always organized within school districts that receive most of their funds from the state.

**Private schools.** Schools that receive most of their funds from private sources such as tuition. They can be parochial schools that are religiously affiliated or schools not affiliated with religion. In the U.S. setting, two common types of private schools include Catholic schools or schools recognized as catering to different populations such as all-girls, all-boys, or college preparatory.

**Charter schools.** Any schools that set out their mission within a charter. Charter schools can operate within a public school district, but are more commonly thought of as operating with public funds at arm's length from a public district or as an individual private school.

**Professional development schools.** Usually public schools that have a rich and robust partnership with a college of education or a university. The intent of professional development schools is to serve as a site to test new ideas and relationships at the school and college levels.

**Schools, colleges, or departments of education (SCDEs).** Units within a university that serve as the principal unit for preparing teachers.

Different agencies and terms are involved in teacher accreditation.

**NCATE.** The National Council for Accreditation of Teacher Education, a non-profit accreditation agency that sets and monitors standards for SCDEs for teacher preparation. In some states, if an SCDE does not meet NCATE requirements, graduates cannot be licensed as teachers. Other states do not require such accreditation.

**INTASC.** The Interstate Teacher and Assessment Support Consortium, an accreditation agency that serves as an alternative to NCATE in some states.

**Licensure, certification, or teacher credential.** A status an individual can receive that recognizes his or her status as a teacher. This status can be conferred by a state department of education or, more rarely, by a teacher professional association within a state.

In addition to individuals, settings, and accreditations, there are experiences described in this book with nuanced meanings.

**Alternative programs.** Alternative pathways to prepare preservice teachers. A popular program is Teach for America, which identifies college graduates and offers intensive short "how to teach" seminars, concluding with placement in a school (see www.teachforamerica.org). Alternative programs can operate in or outside SCDEs.

**Field experiences.** Experiences in which a preservice teacher works in a school classroom. In some cases these field experiences can be in addition to campus course work, corequisite with campus course work, or count as a college course on their own. Fieldwork can be early experiences, in which the preservice teacher largely observes a licensed teacher; intermediate experiences, in which preservice teachers teach in a limited way; or student teaching, in which preservice teachers are responsible for most planning and teaching.

**Teacher preparation programs.** Programs for preservice teachers comprising academic courses focusing on content, such as math, physics, or history; education courses focusing on methods and foundations; and field experience. *See also* **Alternative programs.**

**Supervision.** The process by which preservice teachers are monitored by SCDE and school personnel.

**Supervised field experience.** A field experience monitored by SCDE and school personnel. Typically this includes a field experience specifically targeting the knowledge, skills, and dispositions of preservice teachers in a teacher preparation program. Field experience can occur in the early, middle, or later parts of a teacher preparation program.

# References

Acheson, K., & Gall, M. (1987). *Techniques in the clinical supervision of teachers* (2nd ed.). New York: Longman.

Achinstein, B., & Athanases, S. Z. (Eds.). (2006). *Mentors in the making: Developing new leaders for new teachers.* New York: Teachers College Press.

Achinstein, B., & Meyer, T. (1997, March). *The uneasy marriage between friendship and critique: Dilemmas of fostering critical friendship in a novice teacher learning community.* Paper presented at the annual meeting of the American Educational Research Association, Chicago.

American Association of Colleges for Teacher Education. (1991). *RATE IV: Training teachers: Facts and figures.* Washington, DC: Author.

Anderson, D. J. (1992, February). *A quantitative analysis of student teacher supervision models: Implications for the role of university supervisors.* Paper presented at the annual meeting of the Association of Teacher Educators, Orlando, FL.

Anderson, N. A., & Radencich, M. C. (2001). The value of feedback in an early field experience: Peer, teacher, and supervisor coach. *Action in Teacher Education, 23*(3), 66–74.

Baker, R. S., & Milner, J. O. (2006). Complexities of collaboration: Intensity of mentors' responses to paired and single student teachers. *Action in Teacher Education, 28*(3), 61–72.

Bambino, D. (2002, March). Critical friends. *Educational Leadership, 59*(6), 25–27.

Beck, C., & Kosnik, C. (2002, January/February). Professors and the practicum: Involvement of university faculty in preservice practicum supervision. *Journal of Teacher Education, 53*(1), 6–19.

Beck, C., & Kosnik, C. (2006). *Innovations in teacher education: A social constructivist approach.* Albany: State University of New York Press.

Berliner, D. (1987). But do they understand? In V. Richardson-Koehler (Ed.), *Educators' handbook: A research perspective* (pp. 259–293). New York: Longman.

Birrell, J. R., & Bullough, R. V., Jr. (2005). Teaching with a peer: A follow-up study of the 1st year of teaching. *Action in Teacher Education, 27*(1), 72–81.

Book, C. L. (1996). Professional development schools. In J. Sikula (Ed.), *Handbook of research on teacher education* (2nd ed., pp. 194–210). New York: Macmillan.

Bowman, N. (1979). College supervision of student teaching: A time to reconsider. *Journal of Teacher Education, 30,* 29–30.

Boydell, D. (1986). Issues in teaching practice supervision: A research report. *British Journal of Teacher Education, 2,* 115–125.

Bransford, J. D., Brown, A. L., & Cocking, R. R. (Eds.). (2000). *How people learn: Brain, mind, experience, and school.* Washington, DC: National Academy Press.

Broadley, G. (2000). *Student teacher supervision by telephone.* Paper presented at the Conference of the Australian Association of Distance Education Schools (AADES) and Society for the Provision of Education in Rural Australia (SPERA), Cairns, Australia.

Bryk, A. S., Biancarosa, G., Atteberry, A., Hough, H., & Dexter, E. (2008, December). *Exploring the linkage of changes in teacher practice to improved student learning.* Paper presented at the annual meeting of the National Reading Conference, Orlando, FL.

Bullough, R. V., Jr., & Baugh, S. (2008). Building professional learning communities within a university/public school partnership. *Theory into Practice, 47*(4), 286–293.

Bullough, R. V., Jr., Clark, D. C., Wentworth, N., & Hansen, J. M. (2001). Student cohorts, school rhythms, and teacher education. *Teacher Education Quarterly, 28*(2), 97–110.

Bullough, R. V., Jr., & Draper, R. J. (2004). Making sense of a failed triad: Mentors, university supervisors, and positioning theory. *Journal of Teacher Education, 55,* 407–420.

Bullough, R. V., Jr., Young, J., Birrell, J. R., Clark, D. C., Egan, M. W., Erickson, L., et al. (2003). Teaching with a peer: A comparison of two models of student teaching. *Teaching and Teacher Education, 19*(1), 57–73.

Bullough, R. V., Jr., Young, J., Erickson, L., Birrell, J. R., Clark, D. C., & Egan, M. W., et al. (2002). Rethinking field experience: Partnership teaching versus single-placement teaching. *Journal of Teacher Education, 53*(1), 68–80.

Calderhead, J., & Shorrock, S. B. (1997). *Understanding teacher education: Case studies in the professional development of beginning teachers.* Washington, DC: Falmer.

Carnegie Task Force on Teaching as a Profession. (1986). *A nation prepared: Teachers for the 21st century.* Washington, DC: Carnegie Forum of Education and the Economy.

Carroll, D. M. (2002, April). *Making sense of collaborative learning in a mentor teacher study group: Examining the joint construction and collective warranting of ideas.* Presented at the annual meeting of the American Educational Research Association, New Orleans.

Casey, B., & Howson, P. (1993). Educating preservice students based on a problem-centered approach to teaching. *Journal of Teacher Education, 44,* 361–369.

Castaldi, G. (2006, November). *Western Governors University Teachers College receives NCATE accreditation.* Retrieved November 3, 2006, from http://wgu.edu/wgu/press_release_108.asp

Cazden, C. (1983). Adult assistance to language development: Scaffolds, models, and direct instruction. In R. P. Parker (Ed.), *Developing literacy: Young children's use of language* (pp. 3–18). Newark, DE: International Reading Association.

Cazden, C. (1986). Classroom discourse. In M. C. Wittrock (Ed.), *Handbook of research of teaching* (pp. 432–463). New York: Longman.

Clark, C. M. (2002). New questions about student teaching. *Teacher Education Quarterly, 29,* 77–80.

Clay, M. M. (1991). *Becoming literate: The construction of inner control.* Portsmouth, NH: Heinemann.

Clay, M. M. (2005). *Literacy lessons designed for individuals.* Portsmouth, NH: Heinemann.

Clift, R., Johnson, M., Holland, P., & Veal, M. L. (1992). Developing the potential for collaborative school leadership. *American Educational Research Journal, 29,* 877–908.

Clinard, L. M., Ariav, T., Beeson, R., Minor, L., & Dwyer, M. (1995, April). *Co-operating teachers reflect upon the impact of coaching on their own teaching and professional life.* Paper presented at the annual meeting of the American Educational Research Association, San Francisco.

Cogan, M. L. (1973). *Clinical supervision.* Boston: Houghton Mifflin.

Coleman, J., Campbell, J., Wood, A., Weinfeld, F., & York, R. (1966). *Equality of educational opportunity.* Washington, DC: U.S. Department of Health, Education, and Welfare, Office of Education.

Conant, J. B. (1963). *The education of American teachers.* New York: McGraw-Hill.

Copas, E. (1984). Critical requirements for cooperating teachers. *Journal of Teacher Education, 35*(6), 49–54.

Correia, M. P., & McHenry, J. M. (2002). *The mentor's handbook: Practical suggestions for collaborative reflection and analysis.* Norwood, MA: Christopher Gordon.

Costa, A., & Garmston, R. J. (1994). *Cognitive coaching: A foundation for renaissance schools.* Norwood, MA: Christopher Gordon.

Cruickshank, D., & Haefele, D. (2001). Good teachers, plural. *Educational Leadership, 58*(5), 26–30.

Daane, C. J. (2000). Clinical master teacher program: Teachers' and interns' perceptions of supervision with limited university intervention. *Action in Teacher Education, 22*(1), 93–100.

Dallmer, D. (2004). Collaborative relationships in teacher education: A personal narrative of conflicting roles. *Curriculum Inquiry, 34*(1), 29–45.

Darling-Hammond, L. (1999). *Educating teachers for the next century: Schools for developing a professional.* New York: Teachers College Press.

Darling-Hammond, L. (Ed.). (2000). *Studies of excellence in teacher education: Preparation in a 5-year program.* Washington, DC: American Association of Colleges of Teacher Education.

Darling-Hammond, L., & Sclan, E. M. (1996). Who teaches and why: Dilemmas of building a profession for 21st-century schools. In J. Sikula (Ed.), *Handbook of research on teacher education* (2nd ed., pp. 67–101). New York: Macmillan.

Darst, P., Zakrajsek, D., & Mancini, V. (Eds.). (1989). *Analyzing physical education and sport instruction.* Champaign, IL: Human Kinetics.

Dewey, J. (1938). *Experience and education.* New York: Macmillan.

Dill, V. (1996). Alternative teacher certification. In J. Sikula (Ed.), *Handbook of research on teacher education* (2nd ed., pp. 932–960). New York: Macmillan.

Dirkx, J. M. (2001). The power of feelings: Emotion, imagination, and the construction of meaning in adult learning. *New Directions for Adult and Continuing Education, 89,* 63–72.

Doepker, G. M. (2007). *A study to determine the status of the roles, responsibilities, and practices of university supervisors who serve middle childhood preservice teacher candidates in the state of Ohio.* Unpublished doctoral dissertation. The Ohio State University, Columbus.

Edelman, R. (1998). *The new rules of money: Eighty-eight simple strategies for financial success today.* New York: HarperPerennial.

Educational Testing Service. (2002). *Pathwise classroom observation system: Orientation guide.* Princeton, NJ: Educational Testing Service.

Fairbanks, C. M., Freedman, D., & Kahn, C. (2000). The role of effective mentors in learning to teach. *Journal of Teacher Education, 5*(2), 102–112.

Feiman-Nemser, S. (2001). From preparation to practice: Designing a continuum to strengthen and sustain teaching. *Teachers College Record, 103*(6), 1012–1055.

Flanders, N. A. (1965). *Helping teachers change their behavior.* Ann Arbor, MI: University of Michigan School of Education.

Flanders, N. (1970). *Analyzing teaching behavior.* Reading, MA: Addison-Wesley.

Fountas, I. C., & Pinnell, G. S. (1996). *Guided reading: Good first teaching for all children.* Portsmouth, NH: Heinemann.

Franzak, J. K. (2002). Developing a teacher identity: The impact of critical friends practice on the student teacher. *English Education, 34*(4), 258–280.

Fullan, M. (1993). *Change forces: Probing the depths of educational reforms.* New York: Falmer.

Fullan, M. (1995). The limits and the potential of professional development. In T. R. Guskey & M. Huberman (Eds.), *Professional development in education: New paradigms and practices* (pp. 253–268). New York: Teachers College Press.

Fullan, M. (2007). *The new meaning of educational change* (4th ed.). New York: Teachers College Press.

Fullan, M., Galluzzo, G., Morris, P., & Watson, N. (1998). *The rise and stall of teacher education reform.* Washington, DC: American Association of Colleges for Teacher Education.

Fuller, F. (1969). Concerns of teachers: A developmental conceptualization. *American Educational Research Journal, 6,* 206–266.

Ganser, T. (1996). The cooperating teacher role. *Teacher Education, 31,* 283–291.

Gardner, H. (1993). *Frames of mind: The theory of multiple intelligences.* New York: Basic Books.

Garrett, J. L., & Dudt, K. (1998). Using video conferencing to supervise student teachers. *Technology and Teacher Education Annual, 1998.* Charlottesville, VA: Society for Technology and Teacher Education. (ERIC Document Reproduction Service No. ED 421154)

Gentile, A. M. (2000). Skill acquisition: Action, movement, and neuromotor processes. In J. H. Carr & R. B. Shepherd (Eds.), *Movement science: Foundations for physical therapy* (2nd ed., pp. 111–187). Rockville, MD: Aspen.

Gleissman, D. H. (1984). Changing teaching performance. In L. G. Katz & J. D. Raths (Eds.), *Advances in teacher education* (vol. 1, pp. 95–111). Norwood, NJ: Ablex.

Glesne, C., & Peshkin, A. (1992). *Becoming qualitative researchers: An introduction.* White Plains, NY: Longman.

Glickman, C. D. (1981). *Developmental supervision: Alternative practices for helping teachers improve instruction.* Alexandria, VA: Association for Supervision and Curriculum Development.

Goldhammer, R. (1969). *Clinical supervision: Special methods for the supervision of teachers.* New York: Holt, Rinehart, & Winston.

Goodlad, J. I. (1990). *Teachers for our nation's schools.* San Francisco: Jossey-Bass.

Goodlad, J. I. (1994). *Educational renewal: Better teachers, better schools.* San Francisco: Jossey-Bass.

Goodlad, J. I., Mantel-Bromley, C., & Goodlad, S. J. (2004). *Education for everyone: Agenda for education in a democracy.* San Francisco: Jossey-Bass.

Griffin, G. (1987). Clinical teacher education. *Journal of Curriculum and Supervision, 2,* 248–274.

Grossman, P. L. (1990). *The making of a teacher: Teacher knowledge and teacher education.* New York: Teachers College Press.

Guyton, E., & McIntyre, D. J. (1990). Student teaching and school experiences. In W. R. Houston (Ed.), *Handbook of research on teacher education* (pp. 514–534). New York: Macmillan.

Handal, G. (1999, Fall). Consultation using critical friends. *New Directions for Teaching and Learning, 79,* 59–70.

Hawkey, K. (1995). Learning from peers: The experience of student teachers in school-based teacher education. *Journal of Teacher Education, 46*(3), 175–183.

Hayes, H., Wetherill, K. S., Tyndall, R. E., Hayes, A., Calhoun, D., Nolan, J., et al. (1996, April). *A new vision for schools, supervision, and teacher education: The professional development system and model clinical teaching project.* Paper presented at the annual meeting of the American Educational Research Association, New York.

Holmes Group. (1986). *Tomorrow's teachers: A report of the Holmes Group.* East Lansing, MI: Author.

Holmes Group. (1990). *Tomorrow's schools: Principles of the design of professional development schools.* East Lansing, MI: Author.

Holmes Group. (1995). *Tomorrow's schools of education: A report of the Holmes Group.* East Lansing, MI: Author.

Howey, K. R., & Zimpher, N. L. (1989). *Profiles of preservice teacher education: Inquiry into the nature of programs.* Albany: State University of New York Press.

Howey, K., & Zimpher, N. (1996). Patterns in prospective teachers: Guides for designing preservice programs. In F. Murray (Ed.), *The teacher educator's handbook* (pp. 465–505). San Francisco: Jossey-Bass.

Howey, K. R., & Zimpher, N. L. (1999). Pervasive problems and issues in teacher education, In G. A. Griffin (Ed.), *The education of teachers: Ninety-eighth yearbook of the National Society for the Study of Education* (pp. 279–305). Chicago: University of Chicago Press.

Hudson, J. S. (2002, March). Friday forums. *Educational Leadership, 59*(6), 76–77.

Hunt, D. (1976). Teachers' adaptation: Reading and flexing to students. *Journal of Teacher Education, 27,* 268–275.

Hunter, A., & Kiernan, H. G. (Eds.). (2005). *The reflective mentor: Case studies in creating learning partnerships.* Norwood, MA: Christopher Gordon.

Ingersoll, R. M. (2001). Teacher turnover and teacher shortages: An organizational analysis. *American Educational Research Journal, 38*(3), 499–534.

Isik-Ercan, Z., Kang, H. Y., & Darling, K. (2006, October). *Negotiating new territories: Learning student teacher supervision on the job.* Paper presented at the meeting of the Mid-Western Educational Research Association, Columbus, OH.

John-Steiner, V. (Ed). (1978). *Mind in society.* Cambridge, MA: Harvard University Press.

Kagan, D. M., Freeman, L. E., Horton, C. E., & Rountree, B. S. (1993). Personal perspectives on a school-university partnership. *Teaching and Teacher Education, 9,* 499–509.

Kagan, D., & Tippins, D. (1993). Benefits of crisis: The genesis of a school-university partnership. *Action in Teacher Education, 15*(4), 68–73.

Kahne, J., & Westheimer, J. (2000). A pedagogy of collective action and reflection: Preparing teachers for collective school leadership. *Journal of Teacher Education, 51*(5), 372–383.

Keil, V., Rodgers, A., & Switzer, T. (2005). Crafting an effective professional development school partnership. *The Ohio Journal of Teacher Education, 18,* 25–29.

Kennedy, M. (1999). The role of preservice teacher education. In L. Darling-Hammond & G. Sykes (Eds.), *Teaching as the learning profession: Handbook of policy and practice* (pp. 54–85). San Francisco: Jossey Bass.

Kent, S. (2001, Spring). Supervision of student teachers: Practices of cooperating teachers prepared in a clinical supervision course. *Journal of Curriculum and Supervision, 16*(3), 228–244.

Koerner, M., Rust, F. O., & Baumgartner, F. (2002). Exploring roles in student teacher placements. *Teacher Education Quarterly, 29*(2), 35–58.

Kosmoski, G. J. (1997). *Supervision.* Mequon, WI: Stylex.

Kounin, J. (1977). *Discipline and group management in classrooms.* New York: Krieger.

Kruse, S., Louis, K., & Bryk, A. (1995). *Building professional learning in schools.* Madison, WI: Center on Organization and Restructuring of Schools.

Kuhn, T. (1970). *The structure of scientific revolutions* (2nd ed.). Chicago: University of Chicago Press.

Laffey, J., & Musser, D. (1998). Software and learning systems design for field-based experiences. *Journal of Technology and Teacher Education, 6* (2–3), 193–204.

The largest online grad programs. (2009, May). *US News and World Report: America's Best Graduate Schools, 146*(4), 52–53.

Leavitt, H. B. (Ed.). (1992). *Issues and problems in teacher education: An international handbook.* New York: Greenwood Press.

Lemma, P., Ferrara, M., & Leone, L. (1998). Learning from sharing cultures: Stories from school-university partners. *Action in Teacher Education, 19*(4), 1–13.

LeNoir, W. (1993). Teacher questions and schema activation. *The Clearinghouse, 66,* 349–352.

Levine, A. (2006). *Educating school teachers.* New York: The Education Schools Project.

Lord, B. (1994). Teacher's professional development: Critical colleagueship and the role of professional communities. In N. Cobb (Ed.), *The future of education: Perspectives on national standards in America* (pp. 175–204). New York: College Entrance Examination Board.

Lortie, D. (1975). *Schoolteacher*. Chicago: University of Chicago Press.

Lyons, C. A. (1999). Emotions, cognition, and becoming a reader: A message to teachers of struggling learners. *Literacy Teaching and Learning, 4*(1), 67–87.

Margolis, J. (2008). What will keep today's teachers teaching? Looking for a hook as a new career cycle emerges. *Teachers College Record, 110*(1), 160–194.

Marshall, C., & Rossman, G. B. (1995). *Designing qualitative research* (2nd ed.). Thousand Oaks, CA: Sage.

McCaleb, S. P. (1995). *Building communities of learners: A collaboration among teachers, students, families, and communities*. Mahwah, NJ: Erlbaum.

McEntee, G. H., Appleby, J., Dowd, J., Grant, J., Hole, S., & Silva, P. (2003). *At the heart of teaching: A guide to reflective practice*. New York: Teachers College Press.

McIntyre, D. J., Byrd, D. M., & Fox, S. (1996). Field and laboratory experiences. In J. Sikula (Ed.), *Handbook of research on teacher education*. (2nd ed., pp. 171–193). New York: Macmillan.

Miles, M. B., & Huberman, A. M. (1984). *Qualitative data analysis: A sourcebook of new methods*. Beverly Hills, CA: Sage.

Moir, E. (2003, July). *Launching the next generation of teachers through quality induction*. Paper presented at the State Partners Symposium on Teaching and America's Future, Denver, CO.

Morris, A. K., & Hiebert, J. (2009). Introduction: Building knowledge bases and improving systems of practice. *Elementary School Journal, 109*(5), 429–441.

Mosher, R., & Purpel, D. (1972). *Supervision: The reluctant profession*. Boston: Houghton Mifflin.

National Commission on Teaching for America's Future. (1996). *What matters most: Teaching for America's future*. Washington, DC: Author.

Nokes, J. D., Bullough, R. V., Jr., Egan, M. W., Birrell, J. R., & Hansen, M. (2008). The paired-placement of student teachers: An alternative to traditional placements in secondary schools. *Teaching & Teacher Education, 24*(8), 2168–2177.

Pardini, P. (2000, Spring). Critical friends. *School Administrator, 57*(8), 42–49.

Partington, J. (1982, October). Teachers in school as teaching practice supervisors. *Journal of Education for Teaching, 8*(3), 262–274.

Patton, M. Q. (1990). *Qualitative evaluation and research methods* (2nd ed.). Newbury Park, CA: Sage.

Penlington, C. (2008). Dialogue as a catalyst for teacher change: A conceptual analysis. *Teaching and Teacher Education, 24*(5), 1304–1316.

Piaget, J., & Inhelder, B. (1969). *The psychology of the child*. New York: Basic Books.

Portner, H. (Ed.). (2005). *Teacher mentoring and induction: The state of the art and beyond*. Thousand Oaks, CA: Corwin.

Poser, G. J. (1996). *Field experience: A guide to reflective teaching* (4th ed.). White Plains, NY: Longman.

Reiman, A. J., & Thies-Sprinthall, L. (1998). *Mentoring and supervision for teacher development.* New York: Longman.

Rickard, G. L. (1990). Student teaching supervision: A dyadic approach. *Journal of Physical Education, Recreation, and Dance, 61*(4), 85–87.

Rink, J. E. (in press). *Teaching physical education for learning* (6th ed.). Boston: McGraw-Hill.

Rodgers, A., & Keil, V. L. (2007). Restructuring a traditional student teacher supervision model: Fostering enhanced professional development and mentoring within professional development school context. *Teaching and Teacher Education, 23,* 63–80.

Rodgers, A., & Rodgers, E. (2004). *Scaffolding literacy instruction: Strategies for K–4 classrooms.* Portsmouth, NH: Heinemann.

Rodgers, A., & Rodgers, E. (2007). *The effective literacy coach: Using inquiry to support teaching and learning.* New York: Teachers College Press.

Rodgers, E., Kerbow, D., & Hung, C. (2007, May). *Understanding the Work of Coaching: A Lens for Viewing Classroom Practice.* Paper presented at the annual meeting of the International Reading Association, Toronto, ON.

Rosenshine, B., & Furst, N. (1971). Research on teacher performance criteria. In B. Smith (Ed.), *Research in Teacher Education* (pp. 37–72). Englewood Cliffs, NJ: Prentice Hall.

Rowe, M. (1987). Wait time: Slowing down may be a way of speeding up. *American Educator, 11*(1), 38–43, 47.

Sarason, S. B. (1990). *The predictable failure of educational reform: Can we change course before it's too late?* San Francisco: Jossey Bass.

Schoon, K. J., & Sandoval, P. A. (1997, May). The seamless field experience model for secondary science teacher preparation. *Journal of Science Teacher Education, 8*(2), 127–140.

Sergiovanni, T. J., & Starratt, R. J. (2007). *Supervision* (8th ed.). Boston: McGraw-Hill.

Shulman, L. S. (1987). Knowledge and teaching: Foundations of the new reform. *Harvard Educational Review, 57*(1), 1–22.

Siedentop, D., Tousignant, M., & Parker, M. (1982). *Academic learning time-physical education: 1982 revision coding manual.* Columbus, OH: The Ohio State University, College of Education, School of Health, Physical Education and Recreation.

Simpson, M. (2006). Field experience in distance delivered initial teacher education programmes. *Journal of Technology and Teacher Education, 14*(2), 241–254.

Slick, S. (1998a). The university supervisor: A disenfranchised outsider. *Teaching and Teacher Education, 14*(8), 821–834.

Slick, S. (1998b, September–October). A university supervisor negotiates territory and status. *Journal of Teacher Education, 49*(4), 306–315.

Sprinthall, N. A., Reiman, A. J., & Thies-Sprinthall, L. (1993). Roletaking and reflection: Promoting the conceptual and moral development of teachers. *Learning and Individual Differences, 5,* 284–300.

Stanford, R. L., Banaszak, R. A., McClelland, S. M., Rountree, B. S., & Wilson,

E. K. (1994, February). *Empowering cooperating teachers: The University of Alabama Clinical Master Teacher Program.* Paper presented at the annual meeting of the Association of Teacher Educators, Atlanta, GA.

Stanulis, R. M. (1995). Classroom teachers as mentors: Possibilities for participation in a professional development school context. *Teaching and Teacher Education, 11,* 331–344.

Street, C. (2004, Spring). Examining learning to teach through a social lens: How mentors guide newcomers into a professional community of learners. *Teacher Education Quarterly, 31*(2), 7–24.

Sullivan, S., & Glanz, J. (2000). *Supervision that improves teaching: Strategies and techniques.* Thousand Oaks, CA: Sage.

Supovitz, J. A. (2002, December). Developing communities of instructional practice. *Teachers College Record, 104*(8), 1591–1626.

Supovitz, J. (2006). *The case for district-based reform.* Cambridge, MA: Harvard Education Press.

Tanner, L. N. (1997). *Dewey's laboratory school.* New York: Teachers College Press.

The Teaching Commission. (2006). *Teaching at risk: Progress and potholes.* Washington, DC: Author.

Teitel, L. (1997). Changing teacher education through professional development school partnerships: A 5-year follow-up study. *Teachers College Record, 99,* 311–334.

Thies-Sprinthall, L. (1984). Promoting the developmental growth of supervising teachers: Theory, research programs, and implications. *Journal of Teacher Education, 35*(3), 53–60.

Tobin, K. (1987). The role of wait time in higher cognitive learning. *Review of Educational Research, 56,* 69–95.

Veal, M. L., & Rickard, L. (1998). Cooperating teachers perspectives on the student teaching triad. *Journal of Teacher Education, 49*(2), 108–119.

Vessel, A. M. & Daane, C. J. (2000). *A comparison of cooperating teachers' perceptions of their supervision when involved in a collaborative model or a non-collaborative model.* Paper presented at the annual meeting of the American Educational Research Association, New Orleans, LA.

Vygotsky, L. (1962). *Thought and language.* Cambridge, MA: MIT Press.

Walker, L., Sawyers, L., Scharer, P. L., & Fountas, I. (2008). *Two cases of the use of the Professional Development Support System (PDS2).* Presented at the annual meeting of the American Educational Research Association, New York.

Walkington, J. (2007, October). Improving partnerships between schools and universities: Professional learning with benefits beyond preservice teacher education. *Teacher Development, 11*(3), 277–294.

Walsh, K., & Elmslie, L. (2005). Practicum pairs: An alternative for first field experience in early childhood teacher education. *Asia-Pacific Journal of Teacher Education, 33*(1), 5–21.

Wang, J., & Odell, S. J. (2002, Fall). Mentored learning to teach according to standards based reform: A critical review. *Review of Educational Research, 72*(3), 481–546.

Wilen, W., & Clegg, A. (1986). Effective questions and questioning: A research review. *Theory and Research in Social Education, 14,* 153–161.

Wiles, J., & Bondi, J. (2004). *Supervision: A guide to practice* (6th ed.). Upper Saddle River, NJ: Pearson Merrill Prentice Hall.

Wilson, E. K. (1995, April). *Empowering teachers as full partners in the preparation of new teachers.* Paper presented at the meeting of the American Educational Research Association, San Francisco, CA. (ERIC Document Reproduction Sservice No. ED 385521)

Wilson, E. K. (2006). The impact of an alternative model of student teacher supervision: Views of the participants. *Teaching and Teacher Education, 22*(1), 22–31.

Wilson, E. K., & Readence, J. E. (1993). Preservice elementary teachers' perspectives and practice of social studies: The influence of methods instruction and the cooperating teacher. *Journal of Research and Development in Education, 26,* 222–231.

Wilson, E. K., & Saleh, A. (2000). The effects of an alternative model of student teaching supervision on clinical master teachers. *Action in Teacher Education, 22*(2A), 84–90.

Wilson, K. G., & Daviss, B. (1994). *Redesigning education.* New York: Henry Holt.

Wilson, S. M., & Berne, J. (1999). Teacher learning and the acquisition of professional knowledge. In A. Iran-Nejad & P. D. Pearson (Eds.), *Review of research in education.* Washington, DC: American Educational Research Association.

Winitzky, N., Stoddart, T., & O'Keefe, P. (1992). Great expectations: Emergent professional development schools. *Journal of Teacher Education, 43,* 3–18.

Wittenburg, D. K., & McBride, R. E. (1998, March). Enhancing the student-teacher experience through the Internet. *Journal of Physical Education, Recreation and Dance, 69*(3), 17–20.

Wood, D., Bruner, J., & Ross, G. (1976). The role of tutoring in problem-solving. *Journal of Child Psychology, 17,* 89–100.

Wood, G. H. (1992). *Schools that work: America's most innovative public education programs.* New York: Plume.

Wood, L. H. (1989, August). *Maximizing the development of student teachers during student teaching.* Paper presented at the meeting of the Association of Teacher Educators, Tacoma, WA. (ERIC Document Reproduction Service No. ED312237)

Yates, J. W. (1982). Student teaching: Results of a recent survey. *Educational Research, 24,* 212–215.

Young, J. R., Bullough, R. V., Jr., Draper, R. J., Smith, L. K., & Erickson, L. B. (2005). Novice teacher growth and person models of mentoring: Choosing compassion over inquiry. *Mentoring and Tutoring, 13*(2), 169–188.

Yusko, B. P. (2004, Summer). Caring communities as tools for learner-centered supervision. *Teacher Education Quarterly, 31*(3), 53–72.

Zahorik, J. A. (1988). The observing-conferencing role of the university supervisor. *Journal of Teacher Education, 39*(2), 9–16. (ERIC Document Reproduction Service No. EJ376995)

Zeichner, K. M. (1992). Rethinking the practicum in the professional development school partnership. *Journal of Teacher Education, 43*(4), 296–307.

Zeichner, K., Melnick, S., & Gomez, M. L. (1996). *Currents of reform in preservice teacher education*. New York: Teachers College Press.

Zheng, B., & Webb, L. (2000, November). *A new model of student teacher supervision: Perceptions of supervising teachers*. Paper presented at the meeting of the Mid-South Educational Research Association, Bowling Green, KY.

Zimpher, N. L., deVoss, G., & Nott, D. (1980). A closer look at university student teacher supervision. *Journal of Teacher Education, 31*(4), 11–15. (ERIC Document Reproduction Service No. EJ235491)

Zwart, R. C., Wubbels, T., Bolhuis, S., & Bergen, T. C. M. (2008). Teacher learning through reciprocal peer coaching: An analysis of activity sequences. *Teaching and Teacher Education, 24*(4), 982–1002.

# About the Authors

**Adrian Rodgers** has taught literacy for over 25 years, beginning as a secondary school teacher in Labrador and now as an assistant professor of teacher education at The Ohio State University in Newark, Ohio. He has a PhD in educational studies from The Ohio State University and recently coauthored *The Effective Literacy Coach* for Teachers College Press. His research interests include literacy coaching and supervision, systemic redesign efforts, and professional development.

**Deborah Bainer Jenkins** is professor of curriculum and instruction and interim chairperson of the Department of Health, Physical Education, and Sport Studies at the University of West Georgia. Her scholarly interests include science education, effective instruction, classroom management, and supervision. Her publications appear in numerous journals, including *Teacher Education Quarterly*, the *Journal of Excellence in College Teaching*, the *Journal of Educational Research*, the *Journal of Environmental Education*, the *Journal of Outcome Measurement*, and the *Journal of Research on Rural Education*.

**Robert V. Bullough, Jr.,** is professor of teacher education and associate director of the Center for the Improvement of Teacher Education and Schooling (CITES), Brigham Young University, and emeritus professor of educational studies, University of Utah. His research interests range widely from historical and local studies to a recent ethnomethodological study of teacher work sample scoring ("Proceed With Caution: Interactive Rules and Work Sample Scoring Strategies," *Teachers College Record*, in press). His most recent books include *Stories of the 8-Year Study: Reexamining Secondary Education in America* (SUNY Press, 2007), written with Craig Kridel and winner of the AERA Division B Outstanding Book Award for 2008, and *Counternarratives: Studies of Teacher Education and Becoming and Being a Teacher* (SUNY Press, 2008).

**C. J. Daane** is a professor in the Department of Curriculum and Instruction at the University of Alabama. She is the coordinator of the Elementary

Clinical Master Teacher Program, teaches mathematics education courses and a doctoral seminar on clinical supervision, and has held administrative appointments in the College of Education. Her research interests include mathematics anxiety, preservice teacher competence in mathematics, and clinical supervision effectiveness. She has numerous articles published in academic journals, including *School Science and Mathematics, Action in Teacher Education,* the *Journal of Curriculum and Instruction, Teaching Children Mathematics,* and *The Clearing House.*

**M. Winston Egan** is chair and professor of the Teacher Education Department at Brigham Young University. His research interests include teacher socialization, democracy education, video-anchored instruction, and behavior disorders in children and youth. He has been a contributor to *Teachers College Record, Teaching and Teacher Education,* the *Journal of Teacher Education, Teaching and Learning at a Distance,* and *Behavior Disorders.*

**Cheryl Fortman** holds a PhD from Bowling Green State University in Bowling Green, Ohio, and currently serves as a BGSU graduate off-campus education program officer. Her recent research examines student teacher self-efficacy.

**Virginia L. Keil** is an associate professor in the Department of Curriculum and Instruction and associate dean for undergraduate education at The University of Toledo, Judith Herb College of Education. She also serves as director of teacher education for the university. Her research interests include assessment and evaluation in teacher education and effective models of clinical supervision. She has been published in journals such as *The Teacher Educator, Teaching and Teacher Education,* and the *Midwestern Educational Researcher.* She teaches or has taught courses in reflective practice and teaching in urban settings.

**Jeffery D. Nokes** is a clinical faculty associate in the Department of Teacher Education at Brigham Young University. He is the director of secondary social studies education, teaches methods courses at the undergraduate level, and supervises practicum students and student teachers. His research focuses on history pedagogy, teaching historical literacy, and social studies teacher education. He has published several articles in, among others, the *Journal of Educational Psychology,* the *Journal of Adolescent and Adult Literacy, Teaching and Teacher Education,* the *National Social Science Journal,* and *Reading Psychology.* He has written chapters for the *Handbook of Research on Reading Comprehension* and other books.

**Elizabeth K. Wilson** is a professor in the Department of Curriculum and Instruction at The University of Alabama. Wilson is also the executive director for the Alabama Consortium for Educational Renewal. Her research interests include school-university partnerships, teachers' beliefs, and technology. She has published her research in numerous educational journals and is involved in several grant projects to benefit K–12 schools.

# Index